HOW TO CHOOSE YOUR HAPPINESS DAILY

(Self-Guide of daily habits, rituals, and adjusting your daily view of life)

Fadia Sara Alasmar

Printed in the United States of America

ISBN - 978-1-0878-7820-1

10 9 8 7 6 5 4 3 2-

EMPIRE PUBLISHING

www.empirebookpublishing.com

Acknowledgement

I want to thank my parents for raising me the way they did, and showering me with love and showing me how much hard work pays off in life. I want to thank my husband, who has shown me nothing but support and love and who also made me believe that princess fairytale endings are real. I want to thank my good friend Julia Cox Cason for being such an authentic friend and helping me through this book process. Thank you to Francesca for being so kind and helpful and the rest of the publishing team, that has helped make my dream come true to publish this book and create it the way I want through my own vision. And lastly, I want to thank God, who ever since I was a little girl, has let me throw all my problems on Him, and not once did He ever let me down. I have been shown that life is beautiful, and so I fight every day in troubles, struggles, and sadness to bring the sunlight out in every situation… And the sun does shine everywhere when you let it!

Acknowledgement

Introduction

Writing this book was a way for me to reference all my values, beliefs, and thoughts when I'm down, unmotivated, or not feeling like myself. I'm not a doctor or therapist. But I am a twenty-something-year-old female who seeks out positivity and happiness in this crazy world and in any situation no matter how long it takes me. I created this book sharing my experience in life and what has worked for me to get through the worst of times in my daily life. This book may not cure depression (or maybe it will). This book mainly focuses on how to achieve your long-term happiness and positive lifestyle by making changes in your day to day life. I wrote this book while experiencing several deaths in the family. I wrote this book dealing with family job loss, severe health issues, and personal issues, including unstable financial situations. I wrote this book during a time I lost friends and got hurt by close people in my life. However, this book was also written during the best times of my life with the best experiences. I took the best vacations. I got together with loving family members, improved my career, and started eating healthy and going to the gym regularly. I was gifted with many beautiful things and made beautiful memories with loved ones while writing this book. I learned whatever we are going through will only affect us if we let it. I learned to speak up more and be blunt about my needs, wants, and boundaries. I learned not to be afraid of what people thought about my needs and wants and how I feel. I learned people are more accepting of my boundaries when I enforce them correctly. I learned that it's okay to take a moment and feel my feelings of sadness, worry, and anxiety and to be okay with these feelings as a part of my emotions through life and move on. I also learned to pick myself back up quickly, even if something doesn't work right away. I keep trying to get out of my negative emotions and find a way to chase my happiness and catch it! Here I am showing you my experience and what I've learned in choosing happiness as a daily practice and knowing it's not a destination, but a daily journey. I give you the opportunity in this book to ask yourself many questions and think about how to choose your happiness and never give up on it.

I share with you what to avoid and what to make practice in your daily life to make chasing happiness easier. Please enjoy this journey I have created for you through my own self-awareness and self-practice that has helped me keep my bubbly, positive personality going every day. Write down notes, re-read passages, and highlight sentences that spark interest and motivation for you. Practice. Practice. Practice your happiness journey daily. Make it strong so it will flow easier through your life. Lastly, don't be hard on yourself for failing at anything. Failing is the door that opens you to success and happiness. Embrace it, learn from it, and choose happiness first.

Table of Contents

Acknowledgement.. i

Introduction.. ii

How to Achieve Happiness 1

The Power of Happiness 3

Lies in Gratitude... 3

Creating Your Dream Life.. 8

Into Reality.. 8

Comfort Zone 13

Healthy Happiness - Period (part1)...................................... 18

Healthy Happiness - (part 2) 22

You Look Happy... 27

You First: Self Worth and Self-Care - (part 1: Self Care) 34

Self-Worth - (Part 2) 37

Our Imperfections: Boundaries 44

Our Imperfections: Judgment.. 49

Our Imperfections: Pain 51

Enhance Your Life.. 55

The Simple Life: Money - (part 1) 59

The Simple Life: Life at Its Simplest - (part 2) 65

Single and Happy 76

Romantic Relationships.. 81

Who Inspires You to Elevate Your Life? 91

A Purpose for Life -Faith.. 95

Your Journey Has Just Begun… 98

How to Achieve Happiness

If you want to be happy, you have to be happy on purpose. When you wake up, you cannot just wait to see what kind of day you will have. You have to decide what kind of day you will have. – Joel Osteen

Do you like to feel rich? If you do, what makes you feel rich? If you think going out and buying designer heels is going to make you feel rich, you are wrong. Why you may ask? Because you can buy designer heels on a credit card and be four thousand dollars in debt. That doesn't feel very rich. So how do we make ourselves feel rich in the situation we are in? Maybe you put aside twenty-five dollars a week in your savings from your paycheck. Maybe you eat out less. Maybe you start using coupons whole shopping and limit your shopping altogether. Maybe you a take on a side hustle, like selling your unwanted belongings online. So why do these types of actions you take towards money make you feel rich? Because you're working at building the security of having extra cash saved for yourself. The real feeling of being rich is having money, not buying designer shoes. This same scenario speaks for happiness as well. We feel happiness not necessarily when we go on vacation or finally having a ring on our finger or landing our dream job. Yes, these things can bring you happiness, but your journey us far more important than your destination. Let's say you are finally going to take your dream vacation to Hawaii. Before you get there, you rush through traffic to get to the airport. You complain about how late the plane takes off. You become irritated at how humid Hawaii ends up being. You fight with the hotel staff about how they didn't give you the king-size bed you requested. Are you happy on your vacation? No, because it's not the vacation that's going to make you happy. It's your attitude, your energy, and your outlook towards your vacation. Let's say you enjoy the ride to the airport with your favorite music instead of worrying about beating traffic. You write down a to-do list while sipping coffee on things to do in Hawaii as you wait for your late plane to arrive. You accept the humidity of the island and visualize yourself cooling off at the hotel pool soon. You accept that you won't be sleeping on a king size bed by brushing it off and realizing you won't care where to sleep after a long day of adventures in Hawaii. This type of attitude will give you a happy vacation - Not the vacation itself. And we go back to the idea that feeling rich with your extra cash can buy you expensive shoes, but the shoes cannot really make you feel rich. This is how you achieve happiness.

The Power of Happiness
Lies in Gratitude

"Let us rise up and be thankful, for if we didn't learn a lot today, at least we learned a little. And if we didn't learn a little, at least we didn't get sick, and if we got sick, at least we didn't die. Let us all be thankful"
-Buddha

Two women were working in a boutique. A customer was shopping while listening to the two employees chit-chatting. *"Oh, I just found twenty dollars in my pocket. Too bad I didn't find more." Complained one employee to another. The customer went to the register and bought herself a pretty dress. Before she left, she turned to the employee who found money in her pocket and said. "Well at least you found something - you could have gone about your day and found nothing."*

Gratitude is the foundation of happiness. Going through your day without being aware of all the grateful things that happen in your life will leave you feeling empty and unhappy. Without gratitude, you will always search and desire more without feeling any satisfaction in life. Celebrities, rich people, and people who have power may think they "have it all" but end up on drugs, commit suicide, or fall into depression are the best examples of this. Usually, these people have a big circle of friends, travel the world, wear beautiful clothes, have a beautiful body, and eat at any restaurant they want. Yet, they still fall into life's misery, which is full of emptiness, dissatisfaction, and unhappiness. No matter what you have or achieve, it will not make you happy if you don't enjoy and appreciate every bit of what you have right now. You may say to yourself, *"I do appreciate things in my life,"* or you may say, *"I don't have much to appreciate in my life."* But here's the thing. You can always work on gratitude in your life. Gratitude is a daily practice that you should work on throughout

3

your day. Sometimes you will have to look a little deeper into your day to give gratitude to that day. As quoted by Buddha, *"Let us rise and be thankful"* Basically, the fact that you're breathing is something to be grateful for and is commonly overlooked.

As long as you're breathing, you have the power and potential to enjoy life and choose happiness. The biggest test in your gratitude journey is to be grateful for the bad situations that may occur in your life. For instance, losing your job can be looked at as an unfortunate situation. However, maybe your job loss led you to move in with your sick parent and be able to spend time with them and take care of them. As you take care of your sick parent, you search for another job, and you will usually find that you transition to a new job around the time you finish caring for your ill parent. If you can believe it, life usually tends to work out in this way. A bad situation cannot only be a lesson for you to learn, but it can also end up in your favor. As long as you're not resisting your current situation, whether it is good or bad, and you are able to accept it and even be grateful for it, life seems to work out on its own. Grateful people in any situation they are in, usually hold faith that more good things are coming into their path. The more you are grateful in your life, the more things you will receive to be grateful for. The more you complain about life, the more you will receive things to complain about. This is the law of attraction.

Gratitude for your Annoying Life

Think of all the annoying things in your life. It might be a task, an errand, a chore, or anything else that annoys you. Are you able to think back to that time when that annoying thing in your life was something you were actually looking forward to? Let's think about when we were teenagers. Most teens are waiting for that special moment when freedom is gifted to them. This freedom is symbolized as driving a car! Maybe you were that 16-year-old who couldn't wait to drive around, fill up gas, pick up the milk for mom, or go get a car wash. What happens when we get older? Filling up gas becomes irritating. Going to the grocery store is tiring. Getting the car washed becomes inconvenient. Basically, you're done with adulting. We lose appreciation of the fact that we are able to drive around. We take it for granted because we are used to it and we believe it's our right to drive around and have a car. We forget it's a privilege not everyone has. Next time you are irritated or annoyed to run to the bank, unpack from a vacation, or wash the dishes, think of the reasons to be grateful for what you are able to do through the day and what you are able to provide for yourself. You don't have to force yourself to love everything on your to-do list and all the responsibilities in your life. But learn to be grateful for them and give them your attention and effort for being available in your life. Remember when you dreamed to get to the level you are in. If you really don't enjoy waiting in line at the bank, learn to give gratitude to the fact that you are able to open a bank account and are able to let money flow through to your checking and savings. Everything you do, no matter how repetitive or small you may think it is, adds so much value to your life. Even mopping the floor and putting laundry away has meaning in your life. Mopping your floor symbolizes the fact that you were able to buy the house you couldn't wait to purchase on your own. You are now keeping it clean and taking care of it. Folding laundry and putting it away symbolizes that you have clean clothes for work, going out on the weekends, and vacations! Everything you do in your life is a symbol of some type of achievement or goal you once were striving for. Appreciate all of it, and you will find yourself attracting more things to appreciate and enjoy in your life.

Gratefulness Leads to Fullness

There are so many things in your life to be grateful for. Your appreciation in your life will make you feel fulfilled and satisfied. When you are full, you don't desire to have more as often. When you end up getting more, your life will become more joyous and beautiful. Let's make an example of your living situation. You live in a one-bedroom apartment. You're sitting on the couch with some coffee, flipping through a home magazine, and are inspired to own a beautiful house like the ones in the magazine. However, you are content with your living situation at the moment in your apartment, and you are grateful for it. You show appreciation to your apartment by keeping it clean, decorating it tastefully, and welcoming your friends with pride and warmth in your little home. A year later, you find yourself buying your own house with a pool. You are grateful for the money you saved up to buy the house. You are overwhelmed with joy for the bigger space of the house. You are overwhelmed with happiness to own your own place to live. You leave your old one-bedroom apartment behind and thank it in your heart for sheltering you and making memories for you that will last a lifetime. But you are now ready for your new adventure in your life into a bigger and prettier home. Your gratitude and contentment for everything you have will help lead you to make your life work out the way you want it to.

Practice Your Appreciation Daily

An effective exercise to do on a daily basis to help you train yourself to practice gratitude daily is by using a journal to write down what you are grateful for. You can do this once or twice a day in the morning when you wake up and before you go to sleep at night. Take a few minutes in your pretty journal to write down what you are looking forward to in the morning, like picking up a pumpkin spice Frappuccino before work in October. Before you go to sleep, list all the things you feel grateful for that you did that day. It can be as simple as pushing yourself to the gym and getting in a great workout. Shifting your focus on gratitude and positivity daily has a huge impact on your happiness and a high chance of successfully reaching your goals and dreams. Practice gratitude daily, so it becomes second nature when you go through your day. Think of all the things in your life you are taking for granted. Become aware that everything in your life is a blessing because it can all be taken away from you. Even if we are left in a less ideal

6

situation, search harder for gratitude and appreciation in life, so more will be given to you. This is not a simple task when you are annoyed irritated or upset, which is why a gratitude journal is recommended. Thank yourself for getting up to another day to make the best of it. Thank the Sun for shining. Thank the Earth for turning. Thank the birds for singing. Thank your husband for making you coffee. Thank your dog for licking your face and showing you love. Thank your car for driving you to the mall. Thank your ex for helping you learn what you don't want in your next relationship. Thank your family member who made a rude comment to you for strengthening your self- worth. Thank the car accident for not being any worse. Thank your children when they get on your nerves for teaching you patience. You will always find something to be thankful for. Let it come from the bottom of your heart and let it fill your life with happiness. As quoted by Amy Collette, "Gratitude is a powerful catalyst for happiness. It's the spark that lights a fire of joy in your soul."

Creating Your Dream Life Into Reality

"If you can dream it you can do it." -Walt Disney

Many people don't realize that our home, our car, and our daily visual surroundings have an impact on our success rate and if we are able to manifest our dreams into reality. What we watch, what we read, what we decorate our homes with all impacts our dreams and goals. Let's say a young girl has a dream of having a fashion career. She watches documentaries about fashion. She reads books and follows fashion blogs of well-known fashionistas. She decorates her closet and her room with trends that inspire her. She takes time to dress up every single day. Her friends are into fashion. She gets an internship at a well-known designer company. She works in retail at her favorite designer store while she goes to fashion school. She attends runway shows and makes connections with all types of people that can help her with the industry. Most likely you would say this girl is going to have a successful fashion career. Is she successful because it's easy to have a career in fashion? Absolutely not. But her main focus and priority in life is fashion. She surrounded her whole life bubble around living and breathing this lifestyle. Think about what you would like to change and manifest in your life. Come up with ways to surround yourself with your dream life so you will be successful at receiving your new reality. Here are a few examples of living your dream life as a reality.

Healthy Lifestyle

If you are looking to lose weight or maintain a healthy lifestyle as your main priority, your 3-D vision lifestyle might look like this:

8

Your fridge is clean and organized with plenty of fruits and vegetables. Your kitchen table has a basket full of fruits as a centerpiece. Your kitchen island has clear jar containers filled with dried fruit and nuts for quick, easy snack access. Your bookshelf is full of books that target fitness and a healthy lifestyle. You do research in your spare time about food and fitness to keep yourself motivated and up to date with information. Your closet has a beautiful collection of different sneakers that match your workout clothes that make you feel motivated and fit when you wear them instead of sloppy loungewear. You are surrounded by friends who are health and fitness oriented. You may even have a few trainers and nutrition professionals you keep in contact with. The magazines you subscribe to are dedicated to health and fitness. The main priority in your daily planner is scheduling in your workouts and meal planning. When you are on your phone browsing through Instagram, you follow workouts, food recipes, health quotes, and people who motivate you. You hang fitness and health motivational quotes around your house.

House Entertainer Lifestyle

If you are looking to have a rich social life and become an excellent hostess in your own home, your 3-D lifestyle may look like this:

Your home is always clean and organized. The guest bathrooms are always stocked with essentials like extra towels, toothbrushes, deodorant, face wash, and lotion. You decorate and take good care of the guest bedrooms in your home. Your fridge is stocked with delicious foods. You bake sweets and cakes because you never know who's going to make a surprise visit. You live in an attractive city where family and friends are more likely to visit. You are involved in activities and hobbies like a cooking class or a church where you can meet people and invite them over your home. You have plenty of mugs and plates for your guests. You have a variety of teas and coffee collection. You may invest in etiquette classes or learn from your mother, grandmother, and aunts about hosting in your home.

Romantic Lifestyle

Maybe you are single, or maybe you are married, but you are looking to create more romance in your life. Your dream life may look like this:

You make a list of the qualities you want in your dream partner and keep it close by. Your house is decorated with a romantic and warm vibe like lighting candles at night. You keep flowers on your dining table. You have pictures and artwork of couples walking in Paris, or a couple dancing the tango under the rain. You smile at strangers and give out a positive vibe when you talk to anyone and everyone. You may listen to romantic music when you get dressed in the morning. You visit romantic places in your city even if you are by yourself. You treat yourself to pretty gifts. You may like to watch romantic comedies on the weekend or read romantic books.

Relaxing Lifestyle

Your life is chaotic and hectic. You want to live a slower pace and relaxing life.

Your 3-D lifestyle may look like this:

Your house is neat and clean, with minimal items. You have an area of the house dedicated to meditation, prayer, or relaxation time. You redecorate your bathroom to have a spa-like appearance. You may stock the bathroom with essential oils, face masks, and green plants. You have a playlist on your phone with nature sounds like a waterfall or birds chirping when you get ready in the morning or take a bath. You train yourself to have a softer voice. Your closet may have a collection of comfortable and earth-toned outfits. You minimize your daily tasks as much as you can. Your workouts consist of yoga and walking in nature. You keep stressful phone calls or conversations short, direct, and minimal. You read books and blogs that motivate you to keep your day relaxed. You hang pictures and portraits of the beach or waterfalls in your house. Your phone display says, "Keep calm and carry on."

Vision Board

An increasing popular ritual is being done more and more by people who swear that their dreams are coming true by creating something that is called a vision board. This ritual is usually done at the end of the year before the new year starts. However, you can make one at any time you like. A vision board is a fun, creative, and effective way to visualize all your dreams and goals daily and seeing them manifest into reality.

How do you make a vision board? You can use a poster board and collect magazines or print out words and pictures from your computer that inspire you that are part of your goals. You can make a collage, or you can organize your board into categories like health, career, vacations, and relationships. Whatever your dreams are or whatever inspires you, stick it on your vision board. If words like beauty, shine, sparkle, and glam inspire you, add them on. If you see pictures of fruits and veggies in a magazine, cut them out and use them on your board. Your vision board is something that should make you happy and motivate you every single day. Keep your vision board in a spot you go to daily, like your closet or bathroom. It's important to look at your vision board every day, so your focus will be on your goals and spark inspiration in your life.

Enjoy the process of creating your vision board and adjusting your visual surroundings to your dream life. You may live multiple dreams at the same time. You just need to know if your dream is a romantic and relaxing lifestyle or if you just want to work on your health. You always have the choice of changing your dream life and vision board to adjust your needs and wants. Most importantly, you will need to take a leap of faith that you will manifest your dream life by believing in the magic of the universe without knowing exactly how your vision will turn into reality.

Comfort Zone

"If you think adventure is dangerous try routine. It is lethal"
– Paulo Coelho

How happy are you in your life? Think about it for a moment. How happy are you in your everyday routine? Are you happy with your job? Are you happy with your circle of friends? Are you happy with your house? Are you happy with the clothes you wear? We all have room to improve our lifestyle to the best we can. When you start to feel your energy-draining, you're not motivated in life anymore, you have this uncomfortable feeling within yourself, or you just feel stuck, it's time to step out of your comfort zone and change. It can be about pursuing your hobby as a career, changing your job altogether, changing your circle of friends, changing the country you live in, changing your household lifestyle, changing your finances, it can be anything! But that honestly sounds scary! You want to live safely and comfortably. You may be thinking, you are already used to your crappy hours at work or your difficult living situation, even if that means sacrificing your happiness for your comfortable routine. Comfort and security may sound better than taking risks and jumping into the unknown for the sake of happiness and a better life, but is this really true? Are we really safe when we stay where we are?

Rethinking Comfort and Taking a Risk for Happiness

So why do we want that safe and secure life? Because it feels good to know. It feels good to know that even if you go to work unhappy every day, there's a paycheck waiting for you at the end of the week. It feels good to get out of the house on Friday night, even if you have outgrown your group of girlfriends you have known for years. You may have different lifestyles or not that much in common anymore, but you have known them for so long and feel familiarity when you're with them. It feels good to stay with the boyfriend you have been with for two years, even though he doesn't treat you the same anymore, and you both have different life paths. Think about how long has it been since you have been on vacation? Do you feel anxious thinking about leaving home and going to a foreign place with a different language, even though you dream of traveling the world? Staying in your comfort zone means you know, for the most part, what to expect in your day to day routines. You don't deal with the emotions of risks, failures, the unknown, challenges, and high adrenaline. But is settling for a safe life worth sacrificing your happiness and adventure into what you could achieve? Are you really as safe as you think you are when you stay in your dead-end job? Could your "safe" job possibly surprise you and lay you off or cut your hours without notice? Are your lifelong friends keeping you safe even if you have to tolerate them not treating you nice all the time or not giving you a push to elevate your life? Is your curiosity about the world beyond your little town driving you crazy while you sit at home and wonder what you're missing out on?

Risking it All for Happiness

Usually, your wake-up call alerts you when you become aware that your comfortable routine is hurting you. Instead of keeping you safe, you start to question your life choices. *Why do I feel so drained? Why do I become more irritated easily? Is this really worth the money anymore? I feel so unhappy every time Monday comes around. I don't want to get out of the car and go to work. Why am I still putting up with this crap? Is this my life forever? Can I change this part of my life somehow?* Once we hit rock bottom with a certain part of our life, these emotions and questions will come up daily to help you realize it's time to shift our lives to the better, and change. Unfortunately, the comfort and familiarity of our life routine tries to hold us back because we fear change and failure. We start to

14

push our emotions that are alerting us to change, down the big hole, and dismiss our feelings by saying to ourselves, *"Just suck it up and do it! You have no choice!"* But you always have a choice. We just need to believe we can do it and have the courage to change.

"Whenever we do something outside our comfort zone, good things are bound to happen" – Ashley Hetherington

Step out of the Box

You basically have two ways to step out of your comfort zone box. A baby jump, or a big kid jump. The big kid jump involves you closing your eyes and just jumping off the flight of stairs. And the baby jump is jumping off only one stair at a time. Closing your eyes and making the complete big jump is great because you will accomplish your new life faster, get out of your comfort zone quicker, and face your fears immediately. A baby jump is also great because it makes you jump out of your comfort zone without freaking you out too much about your new life change. Let's say you want a different job. Your baby step might start out as talking yourself into updating your resume. You're not changing your job just yet. You are just glamming up your resume a bit since its been a while. Once you're done with your resume you talk yourself into applying for jobs. You may say to yourself, "In my spare time, instead of watching two Netflix movies, I'll watch one, and I'll just apply to a few jobs. I don't even have to go to the interview. Let me just see if I get a call, just out of curiosity, what I am offered." You may get a call within a few weeks or even a few months for an interview. As long as you keep trying and don't give up, and just stand in the middle of the staircase. To calm your nerves and all the worst-case scenarios going through your head, you remind yourself, you don't have to take any job if you go to an interview. You just want to brush up on your interviews. Before you know it, you are giving in your two weeks' notice and starting a better career for yourself. Taking baby steps down the stairs truly helps you get from point A to point B.

Another example could be as simple as trying a different makeup look you think will be too hard to apply. You can start by talking yourself into applying your regular makeup routine. Once you are done, you realize you're not leaving the house today, so you talk yourself into adding a bold lip color, or winged eyeliner. As you focus on your new look, you many keep trying to perfect it until it comes out the way you want. You don't even notice how many trials and errors you did because you enjoyed the process and hope for a good outcome. Even if you may like your new look, you may fear others will judge you. Well, you like it, don't you? And that's when you will need to always stop yourself from thinking further. Don't continue telling yourself other stories. You like it. You want it. You are happy with it. Then go get it! We can't achieve anything we want in life if we can't face the fears and anxiety of leaving our familiar lifestyle. You will always wish to want what others have or what others do if you don't believe you can achieve the same or better for yourself as well. Nothing will ever get solved in your life, staying in the same box every day, just because you're comfortable.

Your Homework:

- Write down all the things you want to change in your life.
- Write down why it scares you to change, and what's stopping you from changing.
- Write down the reasons you would be happy if you were able to change your lifestyle.
- Create a baby step list that will help you to achieve stepping out of your comfort zone. Make a daily habit of trying to step out of your comfort zone with other things. Changing your direction to work. Making a new complicated recipe. Visit a different town in your area by yourself on a day you wouldn't normally go out. Etc.

RULE: To limit negativity and discouragement, don't share your process with anyone who won't push you to elevate yourself. Stay mysterious!

Healthy Happiness

Period... (part1)

Your health has its category on the influence of your happiness. Your food, your self-care, and your exercise all play an important role in your happiness. Before getting into our fitness and food topic, let's talk about something else that's totally overlooked and not discussed as an important part of our health. However, it has a large impact on your mood, your decisions, and your body. It's called your period.

In her book, Beyond Beauty, Alexandra Villaroel Abrego discusses the importance of the female cycle and how it affects a woman's everyday life. She also explains how some cultures celebrate the female cycle, while many others shun the conversation of it. Many women were not taught how powerful a female's cycle is. Most women know when they get their period it will be painful, tiring and you will wait anxiously for this inconvenience to be over. Many women are embarrassed and don't like to talk about it. Women are also informed about the numerous different birth controls they can use to stop this "inconvenience" that comes once a month. Women are not informed about the power and beauty of their menstrual cycle and how our hormones work in each cycle. The menstrual cycle is not shameful, but a beautiful flow that is part of a woman's body. When you learn each phase of your cycle, you will learn to understand your emotions, be better at decision making, know when to be creative, and become aware when you need to slow down and relax. Find beauty in your body and honor it.

The menstrual cycle is commonly split into four seasons - spring, summer, fall, and winter. Each season follows the phases of your cycle. Winter is known as the menstrual phase (1-6 days). Spring is known as the pre-ovulation phase (7-13 days). Summer is known as the ovulation phase (14-21 days). And fall is known as the luteal phase (22-29 days).

Winter

Winter (1-6 days) menstrual cycle: This is when your uterine lining (your endometrium) sheds and starts to bleed due to no occurring pregnancy. This is the time when your body is in mourning because no baby was fertilized even if you do not want a pregnancy. Your body reacts in mourning by feeling fatigued, pain, headaches, sadness, and feelings of wanting to be alone and withdrawal from the world. Honor this part of your cycle by conserving your energy and relaxing. You probably can't stop going to work and doing your daily activities, but it's important to keep your schedule as light as possible. Do light housework; go to bed early, keep exercise light like doing yoga. Do some journaling and reflecting on your life. This is a great time to have insight into your life and what you want because it's a very vulnerable stage. If you don't live alone, let your household know that you need to slow down and relax for the next few days. Your loved ones will actually help you and encourage you to take time for yourself and get your rest. Watch a movie in bed and snuggle up with a cozy blanket. Allow yourself to rest and slow down. The people who love you will help you and encourage you. Don't rush or try to push yourself through the process. Honor what your body is asking from you.

Spring

Spring (7-13 days) pre-ovulation cycle: This phase of your cycle is when the eggs start to mature, and your estrogen increases. If you think about spring, you may visualize flowers blooming, the grass growing, weather getting warmer, and birds chirping. Just like spring gives off growth and positive vibes, so do you. You will start to feel energized, positive, and be open to learning and growing in this phase especially. Honor this phase by trying a new hobby like a dance class or foreign language course or new lipstick color. Brainstorming for a new project or getting more involved in work events is best during this phase. Our appetite is suppressed due to the increase of estrogen, which makes it easier to fill your body with earthy foods like greens, fruits, and protein.

Summer

Summer (14-21days) ovulation: This is the phase where our body starts getting ready for fertilization. We release an egg into the fallopian tube and into our uterus. Our hormone levels are high, our energy is high, and our mood is high. Its summer, the sun is shining all day long. You will feel sexiest in this phase and notice you take care of your looks more to appear more attractive. Honor this phase by living your life to the fullest. Exercise hard. Work harder. Socialize with friends and strangers. Wear a flirty dress. Plan date nights with your partner or go on dates at this time.

Help a friend out or do some volunteer work. Basically, your energy is at its highest, so take advantage to be productive, fun, and sexy.

Fall

Fall (15-29 days) premenstrual cycle: This phase is about winding down before the winter. During fall, the weather gets cooler, the leaves on the trees fall to the ground, and animals prepare for hibernation by eating extra food and storing it as fat. Fall comes in preparation for winter, so you will have many emotions that come up during the premenstrual phase that leads you to your menstrual phase. In this part of the cycle, you will start to want to withdraw from people, feel more irritation, feel more emotional, and have a bigger appetite. Honor this phase by accepting your mood swings and mixed feelings. Become aware and journal about how you feel. You can give a little warning to your household like your partner to keep the conversations light at this time to avoid conflict and fights that may occur due to the emotional roller coaster you may experience. When you are aware of when you are in this phase, you will be able to control and understand your emotions more and just be okay with them. This is a great time to pull away from social events and friends for a little while and focus on other tasks. Cleaning, organizing, and un-cluttering your house and your life are encouraged in this phase due to your enhancement to details and getting your life in order. It will also keep you busy when you start to withdraw from socializing. Just like animals eat excess food and store it to prepare for hibernation, you will also feel food cravings and your appetite opening. Instead of resisting, try to eat comfort foods in moderation without feeling guilty. It's important to rest and not judge yourself for your open appetite and mixed emotions.

As you pay attention and become more aware of your cycles, you will notice that not every woman's cycle is the same. It's merely a guideline to help you understand your own cycle. You may learn how to tell what day and what phase you are in due to your body's emotions, needs, and wants. The more you become in tune with your body, the more you will be able to know what phase of your cycle you are in without even counting days. Remember, never be embarrassed or ignore your phases. Our cycle is part of our feminine beauty. We can have better control of our emotions and our life as we listen to our bodies and honor each phase it goes through. Celebrate Mother Nature within yourself instead of shunning it so you will always be in tune with your body, giving it its needs and wants.

Healthy Happiness
(Part 2)

"Health is like money. We never have a true idea of its value until we lose it" - Josh Billings

Food is the center of not just your weight but also your mood, energy, and your happiness. Food can cause fatigue, headaches, stomach aches, rashes, and other diseases. But food can also give us energy, heal our skin, heal our organs, and prevent diseases. It's in your hands what foods you choose to put in your mouth and what type of nutrients you want to give your body. As we get older, signs of aging start to show. Allergies you may have never had, or you didn't know you had before, start to develop more. You decide with the way you eat and how much exercise you do, whether you reverse aging, and limit health problems, or you advance them. Having a healthy slimming body with glowing skin is hard work. Very hard work. We live in a society where donuts are served as a morning breakfast instead of fresh fruits. There is no way around looking your best and feeling your best. You have to work on yourself every single day. Once you achieve your ideal body, you keep going. You never stop taking care of your body. It's a continuous journey that we have to make a habit of every day. It's part of your self-care and self-worth. It's about putting yourself first and overcoming the impossible. There are plenty of obstacles that may arise and get in the way of taking care of your health. Don't let difficult situations that you can overcome with dedication and hard work be your excuse not to heal and take care of your body.

Prepare Your Body

The first step to taking care of your body is getting to know your body more. You can take a trip to the Drs. Office and ask your Dr. to check if you are deficient in any vitamins. You can also check if you have any allergies to certain types of foods. Have your Doctor look into any health concerns you may have as well, like high cholesterol, diabetes, or thyroid problems. Another way to prepare yourself is by getting to know food. What are the health benefits of your fruits and veggies? What are those weird ingredients you can't pronounce in your processed snack foods? Research everything. Forget about what you have been told about healthy and non-healthy foods. Do your own research. Many food advertisements will tell you to eat or drink more or less of something for your health. People and businesses can even make healthy foods look dangerous due to misinformation or to sell you their products. Remember, people may believe false information and businesses want to sell their products. So really take the time to learn the science and facts about what you eat. This will help you start somewhere and help you focus on your health more.

Exercise

You must find time for your exercise routine at least 3-4 times a week, if not more. It doesn't matter if it's in the morning, late at night, on your work break, or during the weekend. You need to fit in your workouts weekly. Money is no excuse. You can always exercise for free in many ways. You can watch free videos online to exercise at home with an instructor. You can walk outside or take a hike in the park. There are so many options for a free workout session. If you prefer signing up at the gym, start cutting out restaurant and shopping trips on the weekend to save for a gym membership. Do not feel like you have to stick to one routine of exercise. Switch up your exercise routine, so you don't give up and get bored. You may be interested in a spinning class for a while. Then you may sign up for a dance class. The next month you may get into cardio and weight lifting. It's all about how you feel you want to move your body. Give yourself some variety so you will enjoy keeping in shape. Don't let a health problem be your excuse either. Many health problems can actually be healed with exercise and a healthy diet. Even joint pain and muscle pain can be improved by exercising and strengthening your body. You may have to work harder and research what foods may improve your disorders and what foods to avoid. Without good health, you cannot work, enjoy life, or feel good from the inside and out. Taking care of your body is not a luxury. It is a necessity. It is the difference between spending your days from doctor to doctor or vacationing with your family and exploring the world in good health.

Listen to Your Body

When you start to listen to your body, you can drastically change how you look and how you feel in ways you never imagined. Listen to how your body reacts to the food you eat. Do you feel fatigued? Does your stomach hurt? Do you feel constipated? Do you break out into bumps and rashes? You will come to find out many of these problems will be linked to any stress and food that does not digest well in your body. It may take some time to understand your health. However, the more you take notice of your body, the more you will be able to recognize the normal and abnormal feelings you have after you eat or drink. You can even create a daily journal writing down the foods you eat throughout the day and the amount of food you eat. You can also at the end of each meal or the end of each day write down how you feel and what type of body reactions you had that day. Enjoy the process of getting to know your body and how it wants to work well for you. Listen to your body and treat it right every single day.

The Real Meaning of Food

Food is beautiful! We use food to fill our bodies with energy, for social gatherings, to satisfy our cravings, and much more. We like to eat what pleasures us and makes us happy. Taste buds were created for us to enjoy food. However, these days due to heavy stress in our daily lives, people tend to look at food more as pleasure and a stress reliever rather than fuel for the body. Again, you must remember, businesses want to sell addictive and tasteful foods to us for their pockets to be full. Don't fall into that trap and forget what real nutritious food tastes like and why it was created in the first place. Replace the idea that food is fuel for your body. Stop telling yourself you deserve fast food on your way home from work every day because you work hard and have long days. Your body does not actually deserve little nutrition and unhealthy food. It deserves vitamins and minerals to keep your energy going. You deserve healthy glowing skin and a fit body. Fuel your body with natural foods you love that were created by Mother Nature, not man-made. Your body will show you appreciation when you look in the mirror and love what you see or when you can energetically finish your tasks for the day. Let your healthy choices give you happiness and pleasure from the inside out.

The Others

What about the others? Other people, other friends, other family members? It's probably going to happen… Other people will tempt you to go out to restaurants with them and make bad choices, eat that piece of cake, or skip the gym to go to the movies. This is where your boundaries will show how strong they are because the answer has got to be "Thank you, but no!" You need to be strong to stand up for yourself and your new transition in life. The hardest situation to be in is when you're the only family member in the house living a healthy lifestyle. People may leave their unhealthy snacks on the table. The pantry might be full of junk food. People may not even be very supportive of your new lifestyle. But it doesn't matter. It's your body. It is also your decision whether you let that bag of chips in the pantry tempt you or not. You may even be able to have your own designated cabinet for your healthy food so you can open that evil pantry less often. Some people may be supportive and some may not. Grandma's feelings may be hurt if you don't eat her homemade Bundt cake.

You may find ways to be creative in the way you say no without hurting anyone's feelings. Let's say you have a family member, despite being supportive in healthy eating and exercise, would still try to get you to eat desserts or sweets they make. You may tell her you're not craving sweets right now, and you will try it when your cravings kick in. Don't waste the calories on food you're not craving at the moment. Wait until you have that urge when you can't resist anymore and eat whatever you're craving in moderation. "I'm so full I can't even take a bite" or "I'm not a cake person" are all statements that may help you deal with awkward situations to keep your boundary strong and your body happy.

Living a Healthy Lifestyle

As you may have heard, again and again, a healthy lifestyle blossoms from daily healthy habits. It's not an overnight miracle. It takes lots of time and patience to get to where you want to be. And once you get there, you must not go back to old habits, because your old habits will lead to disappointment and all your hard work goes to waste. So, plan on enjoying healthy foods daily, skip extra calories that mean nothing to you. Listen to your body. Find exercises and transition your workouts to how you feel and what you're in the mood to do. Be firm with your boundaries with others. And enjoy the results of a happy, healthy body!

You Look Happy

"You can have anything you want in life if you dress for it" – Edith Haul

Glow-getter (noun) – A driven busy gal who strives to achieve her goals in life while attaining a beautiful glow both inside and out.

Everyone is attracted to beauty. We are attracted to flowers, the sunset, tropical beaches, exotic food, and all different kinds of people. Think of what your eyes enjoy looking at. It could be pretty colors, glowing skin, a sparkly dress, a cute baby or animal, or your friend's long black silky hair. Life is full of beautiful things to look at for us to enjoy. We should enjoy the same feeling when we look at ourselves in the mirror every day. You are worth looking at yourself every day and loving what you see in the reflection. No matter how tired, how busy, or how lazy you may feel. There is nothing that should stop you from feeling attracted to yourself from the inside and out.

"On a bad day, there's always lipstick." – Audrey Hepburn

If you had your own business, how would you run it? How would you make it stand out? Let's say you owned a bakery. You create pretty bows on the box for the sweets to go. You make sure your baked goods always look presentable and delicious. You may decorate the bakery with pictures and fun themed colors to make your shop more attractive. You may hire employees who are kind and always have a bright smile on their face. You put all this hard work and effort into every detail of the shop. You want more people to come and buy your baked goods. You want others to talk about how delicious the cookies are and how friendly the employees are. You want to make a great impression for your shop.

What if you were that bakery shop? You are your own brand who needs to show the world who you are and be proud of your hard work and success. You choose how you would like to be perceived in front of others. Your physical appearance is your own brand. You should work day and night to make yourself as presentable as possible. You even need to work on the small details like putting lotion on your body to keep your skin from drying or shaving your legs even in the winter when no one can see. A business owner may be tired of working hard every day. She may also have other commitments then the bakery like family and hobbies. However, a business owner will never neglect her shop. She won't give in to the obstacles and struggles that come her way. So, don't neglect yourself. You are the bakery. Sprinkle yourself with glitter. Wear pretty bows. Smell as sweet as pie. Bring others to smile with you and enjoy your company. You are worth taking care of yourself as first priority.

You Don't Care than I Don't Care

If you are the type of person who does not care about their looks or who does not care five days out of the week, then you are not taking yourself or your life seriously. When you start your day with, "I don't care how I look," your whole day will follow the same way. Magically, your attitude about your looks will translate into: I don't care about my performance at work. I don't care about what I eat. I don't care about seeing my friends tonight. I don't care where life takes me. When you start to care about your appearance, you begin to care about everything else. You care more about putting effort at work. You care about your nutrition choices. You care to go the gym after work. You care to meet up with your friends at night. You care to improve your life. You will know the difference in how you feel and how different your days are, when you fix yourself up in the morning ready for the day, or when you just don't care!

Work on Your Beauty Daily

It's important for you to put on an outfit that makes you feel happy every single day. It's also essential that you eat healthy and excise to be confident in your body. You don't need a lot of makeup, and you don't need expensive clothes to feel amazing. Your best weapon is exercising, eating healthy, and putting in some time in the morning for your appearance. When you feel confident in your body, radiate healthy skin and a healthy glow, you have the power to make the cheapest foundation and the cheapest blouse look more expensive than any designer name you may own. Get into the habit of putting yourself together. Wear your favorite mascara. Put on your favorite heels or whatever makes you feel fabulous. Leave behind the idea of saving your best items for special occasions. Where your best things right now and treat yourself to new things when those special occasions come up.

No Excuse

Whatever you prioritize and focus on in your life will be the major part of your lifestyle. If you create in your mind that you are too busy to put yourself together every day, then you will not find time to make yourself pretty. If you are too tired to exercise, then your life will be tiring. If you are too lazy to meal prep for the week, then your week will be full of laziness. Once you stop prioritizing and believing in being too busy, lazy, and tired in your life, then you can start achieving what you want. If you would love to start your morning with putting on your makeup every day, then that should be your priority, and you should turn it into a morning ritual. Even if you have to sacrifice certain things or change your lifestyle around a little bit, your priorities should get done first. How amazing does it feel to put yourself together in the AM? How much love do you feel for yourself when someone compliments how amazing you look or how amazing you feel when you pass by your reflection? How self-conscious and down do you feel when you don't care for your physical appearance? Choose to put music on while you do your hair and makeup and get dressed nicely every day. If you have an early appointment, get up earlier and dress well for the day. If you feel lazy, talk yourself into only putting on mascara and the next thing you know, you may find yourself matching your earrings to your shoes. If you are staying home all day, tell yourself how amazing it will feel to pick out cute loungewear clothes, put your hair up in a combed ponytail with some mascara and lip gloss. You know you will be much more productive at home, and you won't be shy to answer the doorbell if it rings. Dress up every day, and don't let any excuse keep you from presenting your best self, even if the only one who will see you that day is your poodle.

Simplify Your Appearance

In today's world, we are so blessed with the endless options of products and clothing we are able to choose from. We have the freedom to try different moisturizers, makeup, and clothing styles until we find what we love. Running to the store or purchasing whatever your heart desires online has never been easier. Although variety and easy access to anything we want is a huge blessing, it is also a huge disadvantage as well.

When you have a moment, go to your room and observe your belongings. Split your stuff up into categories like haircare, skincare, makeup, fragrance, jewelry, clothes, shoes, purses, etc. You can split your categories to be even more specific if you want. When you look at all your stuff, are you happy with what you own? Do you feel like you have a problem expressing yourself with what you own even though you have a variety of everything? Are you still searching for items that may satisfy you even more than what you already have? The easy access to owning anything we want and the variety of choices we have to pick from are all amazing blessings in today's world. However, we are confused more than ever when we purchase the items that we think will make us beautiful, feel fabulous, and add value to our lives. There are endless of advertisements from bloggers, people we follow on social media, and our friends around us who expose us to the newest and best thing to have. The variety of choices we have is not leading us to choose the best things that work for us, but to create more options for us to own and more material things to have "just in case." We may think when we watch women on social media and watch our friends imitate owning drawers of makeup and skincare, and filling their closet up to the brim is what we are supposed to do. We may believe we are worth all that we own. However, we lose ourselves through all the options we have and forget about what we originally love and what makes us feel good. We end up following our desires to have more things that don't really add value to our lives. Let's clean out the clutter that is hiding who we really are and go out and purchase what we really love. Let's awaken ourselves to the world of fashion and beauty and not allow money-making businesses to rob our happiness and confuse our choices.

The famous book, *Life Changing Magic of Tidying Up by Marie Kondo*, emphasizes throughout the decluttering journey to only keep what sparks joy. The book also focuses on thanking each item you own even if you never wore it or used it. Basically, the idea is to truly appreciate what you own and what things the universe has provided for you. If you can't appreciate what you have, you will always be in search of more. The goal with representing ourselves is not about how many clothing items we own, but how beautiful each purchase we have made for ourselves, enhances our looks and personality. You want to get to the level of owning all beautiful items with nothing extra or any distracting clutter. Let's say you own multiple perfumes and body sprays. However, there is one particular perfume that you get compliments on all the time by your husband, the stranger at the grocery store, and your great aunt. You love that perfume, and you feel fabulous when you wear it. But since you have so many other ones, you feel guilty and try to use up everything you have. Your signature scent gets lost in the pile of perfumes you own. When you clutter up your life in this way, you are losing each day you don't spray yourself with your signature scent, confidence, compliments, a hug that lasts a second longer, and conversations with strangers that may lead to unexpected opportunities. You are too busy and stressed trying to use up an expensive perfume that a YouTube blogger you admire wears, but doesn't really blend in with your body chemistry. It's a waste of time, money, and happiness to own so many things that conceal your favorites and push them to the back of your drawer, shelf, or closet. Here is another example of acknowledging and valuing your belongings. If you watch beauty bloggers, you will, at some point, hear them say, "I found an old favorite" or "I forgot how much I used to love this item." Why are women who have already discovered what they love keep buying more items and losing the items they know they already love? Yes, it is their job to advertise new products so we can learn about them before we even buy them. However, we are getting sucked into trying those products that we don't need because that's of te beauty industry business! It is chaos to our souls when we cannot express our beauty or enhance our appearance when we are overwhelmed with our purchases.

Your homework:

Find value in your appearance again. First, find value in what you already own and forgot about. Enjoy the process of finding items that will enhance your appearance. Get up every day and dress up no matter how your feeling. Celebrate the items you already own and love by keeping them clean, tidy, and using your items like a piece of décor for your closet and drawer. Don't just fling your clothes into the closet. Also get into the habit of celebrating your new purchases that you're bringing into your life. Make shopping a special event instead of a weekly habit. Special shopping occasions helps you appreciate what your hard-earned money is spent on and enhancing the value of your items. When you start to appreciate your favorite items and turning them into your signature style, you begin to realize you don't need collections of items, and you stop searching for what you may already have. Get a journal and write down what colors inspire you. What type of clothes enhances your body? What skincare works well with your skin? Is there a particular color lipstick that makes you feel beautiful and you receive compliments on it often? These things enhance your appearance and make you feel confident and beautiful. So, dust off your favorite shoes. Pull out your favorite night cream. Wear your cute matching PJs daily, instead of saving them for a girl's night sleep over. And fall in love with your reflection in the mirror.

You First: Self Worth and Self-Care

(Part 1: Self Care)

How often do you put yourself first before others? Do you find taking care of your needs and wants before your kids, parents, or friends to be a selfish act? Do you believe we are living on this Earth to help others as much as we possibly can? Do you feel guilty or worry what others will think of you if you take care of your needs first?

When you put yourself first, you are taking care of your needs, wants, and your happiness before anyone else. Putting yourself first means you are practicing self- care daily. Doing what you love instead of what you have to do, and saying no when something doesn't feel good is all part of taking care of yourself. More often than ever, we are putting ourselves on the back burner while putting others in front of us. It is a beautiful feeling when we help people. You may feel joy helping your boss, a friend, or a family member, or an organization. However, it's not okay to help them when you need help yourself. Another reason we may not feel self-care is important, is because we may feel guilty taking care of ourselves before our loved ones. When you have a long to-do list to finish, or you feel it's more important to overwork yourself to provide for your household, you may feel guilty to take care of yourself. Your husband, or kids, or your parents need you. There is too much stuff to get done. You can't be thinking about fixing your hair or taking the time to read a book. However, these are invalid excuses. There's no excuse that comes before self-care.

Balance Self Care in Your Life

It is essential that you balance self-care in all areas of your life. This includes your appearance, your sleep, your body, your health, and your mind. When we don't take care of ourselves, or we don't eat well, and we don't clear our minds, we will feel disorganized, anxious, irritated, and tired. This can possibly lead a person to depression. Lack of self-care will drive us into making mistakes, not giving our one hundred percent effort to help others, and not thinking clearly. We forget that when we put effort into self-care, it does not take away from our time to do "more important stuff." Self-care actually helps enhance our productivity level in everything we do. For example, if you have back pain, and your Doctor recommends for you to go to physical therapy twice a week, is it better for you to say you will deal with the pain and use the time you would have spent in physical therapy to get things done on your to-do list? Or is it better for you to spend that hour going to physical therapy and being more comfortable doing your tasks since you are managing your pain?

Self-Care is Very Attractive

When you take the time to put yourself together in the morning, take part in your favorite hobbies, and take care of your overall health while balancing other parts of your life, people will be intrigued and inspired by you. Society is attracted to the people who take time to travel, learn a new language, read books, take dance and cooking classes and balance their lifestyle at the same time. People get sucked into their to-do lists and daily life routines. They forget that self-care is just as important as their commitments in life. Make sure your taking the time out of your busy life to do what you love and take care of yourself. Sometimes that might mean just sitting on the couch with your dog and doing absolutely nothing. Self-care is refreshing for the soul and makes you a vibrant person. You will feel hopeful and motivated to continue improving your life with purpose.

Bad Days are Bad days- A Cozy Day for yourself

Sometimes it's recommended that if you are in a bad mood to surround yourself with people who uplift you or talk to someone you trust. Although this is true in some situations, this is not always something your soul needs. Ask yourself, Will talking to someone help you feel better, even if you don't share with them what exactly is bothering you? You may just need some company? If the answer is yes, then absolutely grab a cup of coffee and meet up with that special someone who will give you an energy boost. However, if you are feeling impatient, irritated, or angry, and you may end up taking it out on your loved ones, sometimes the best thing to do is isolate yourself and take some time alone for yourself. Let your household know you're upset or angry, and you need a little time to cool off. This way, you don't make the mistake of saying something you don't mean or spreading your energy to others. Usually, people will understand and respect your needed space. You may just need one of those days in your pajamas and watching Netflix movies all evening with some popcorn and chocolate. Or you may want to put a facial mask on and lay down with some nature music playing in the background.

What do you do when you are trying everything you can to get rid of your bad mood and negative energy, and you can't shake it off? Embrace it! It can be frustrating in certain circumstances to try to be positive and bring yourself out of a bad mood. Sometimes you just need to accept your low energy. Become aware of your feelings right away. Once you have accepted your bad mood, you have the best opportunity to take care of yourself and give yourself some self-love. Taking care of yourself will help you deal with your negative energy without going against your feelings. Honor how you feel and tell yourself it's okay and part of being a human to have these feelings in a world that's not perfect. It's okay to allow yourself to be in a bad mood, but don't stay in that energy for too long. After you have given yourself love and kindness, you need to pick yourself back up and get ready for a fresh new start.

Self-Worth
(Part 2)

"I want you to believe me when I say: Your worth does not come from your relationship status, your body figure, your career, your parents' approval, you're busy and productive schedule, your selfless acts of kindness, your house, your bank account, your friends, your lifestyle and whatever else you think, or what society thinks make up your worth. Your worth comes from you...just being the real authentic you. No judgments allowed from yourself or others." – Love from Me, the Author!

When we were babies, the whole world thinks we were just so cute and so adorable. We were fed, our diapers were changed, and our parents played with us and made funny faces at us to try to get us to laugh. As babies, everyone wants us to be happy and keep us smiling, so we don't cry. What happens as we grow older? When we make a mistake, our parents may yell at us. Kids make fun of us at school. We experience the horrible feeling of getting a bad grade on a test. We experience the pain of a best friend backstabbing us. Society tells us what we can and cannot do. We experience failure, disappointment, and betrayal from others and within ourselves. Our self-confidence deteriorates overtime when we let anything exterior affect us. Society tells us we are worth a three-thousand-dollar credit card. We are worth a designer handbag, or we are worth minimum wage.

We start to measure our worth with what we can afford and how people judge us. We even get to a point where we over-schedule our lives with hobbies, activities, events, and overtime at work to prove to others we are worth the oxygen we are breathing. People compete with each other, who has a busier and more tiring schedule than the other. Some even try to find their worth in their relationships. They may feel worthless if a man breaks up with them. Some people's self-worth depends on their relationships, only when family and friends praise their talents and approve of their life. We will then feel we are worth something when we get the approval we are looking for. We are constantly putting our worth in other people's hands, which is very unfair and very wrong.

We need to stop asking ourselves, will they think I'm worth it? You need to start treating yourself with love, respect, and value.

Practicing Self-Worth Daily

Your first step to practicing self-worth daily is to start believing you are worth everything you desire, just the way you are. You need to stop feeling guilty for taking vacations from work. You need to stop listening to friends and family who put you down and criticize your dreams and goals in life. You need to stop looking for the wrong attention from men to make you feel you are worth something.

Including in your daily life, something like saying affirmations daily is such a key in having a positive attitude. When you use affirmations, you are constantly repeating to yourself positive statements throughout your day, keeping your mind strong and optimistic. When you wake up in the morning, look in the mirror and tell yourself you are worth it. When you are debating on buying the organic carrots or buying the cheaper veggies, whisper to yourself, you are worth the healthy organic option. When you are debating on going into work sick or calling out to rest, tell yourself you are worth the day off to get better and heal. If you want to take a risk and follow your passions or stay in your job that you're only passionate about for your paycheck at the end of the week, tell yourself you are worth taking a risk and finding your career happiness. Once you start saying it to yourself and then acting upon your new self-worth, it will become easier to accept a life you never thought you were worthy of.

It's not selfish to love yourself, take care of yourself, and to make your happiness a priority. It's necessary. – Mandy Hale

Stop the Guilt Trips

When you work tirelessly to put your kids first, your husband first, your boss first, or your friends first, what do you notice usually happens? You probably feel like no one appreciates you. You feel your hard work to make them happy goes unseen most of the time. Here is the big lesson in this situation. No matter how hard you try to make others happy, it will not make a difference in your relationship if you are not happy. As long as you are helping others because you think they will like you more, or you feel bad because they begged you for your help, basically, you are putting their happiness first and yours last. Don't waste your time and energy, keeping others happy. It's not your job. Your job is to find your own happiness first and then help others when you are able to along the way.

Keep Within Yourself

One aspect you need to pay attention to is being more mysterious with your life. You don't always need to explain yourself to people. You don't need to share all your dreams or goals. Mystery keeps people guessing about you and respect your private life. They may try to be nosy but be kind, firm, and limit what you say in front of people. As wisely stated by the famous French Philosopher and writer, Voltaire: *"Each player must accept the cards life deals him or her. But once they are in hand he or she alone must decide how to play the cards in order to win the game."* This way, you don't have people's negativity and unwanted opinions getting thrown at you and overwhelming you. You also need to practice listening to how you feel. If you want to sit at home and read a book rather than go to the movies with your friends, then do just that! You can practice being more mysterious in these types of situations as well. Instead of telling your friends why you don't

39

want to go to the movies and opening the door for them to change your mind when you really don't want to, you can simply say you are unable to go out this week maybe next week without giving any explanations. Become more aware of what you say and who you say it to. Part of your self-worth is limiting exposure to your life and sometimes that means, keeping what you say, short, simple, and sweet.

Value Your Time and Energy

Learn not to invest your whole life for people. Appreciate your time and energy instead of searching for someone to appreciate you. Start saying no to any favors you're not happy to do or any promises you can't happily keep. Develop a habit to ask yourself questions like, "If I did this favor for a friend, is that really what I want to do, or am I doing it out of guilt?" It is easier and more convenient for anyone to have you do everything. They may get upset if you don't put their needs first, especially if they are used to you putting their needs first and saying yes to everything. But, is that what you want? Do you have time to put others before yourself? Are you happy giving a helping hand, or are you burning out? Do you need to show yourself more love? How can you put yourself first and enjoy it without feeling guilty or selfish?

What Do Your Boundaries have to do with Your Self-Worth?

How often do you allow people to step over your boundaries? Your boundaries are the red flags that you don't like people to cross over. It doesn't feel good, and it does not bring you happiness when your boundaries are crossed. When we put ourselves first, we are taking care of our needs, our wants, and our happiness before anyone else. Some people may not like that. Some people may even be jealous. Some people will make you feel bad about it, which starts up the guilt trip. You may even find that you are not aware of what your boundaries are. You may have the tendency to make yourself uncomfortable so you can make others happy. You get burned out, always thinking about other people's needs and wants. You may do things you don't want to do to make others happy. You keep your mouth shut to please people. You may not engage in certain activities and hobbies for yourself so that you could be there for others. This is not self-care. This is not loving yourself. This is not putting yourself first. This is not chasing your happiness. This is people taking advantage of you and using up your valuable energy. This is letting people cross your boundaries.

Balance You First Vs. Helping Others

It's a beautiful feeling to help other people in your life. The lesson in this chapter is not to stop helping people all together and only being selfish. The lesson is to make sure you are happy first in whatever you are doing. We are not putting ourselves first enough, which is resulting in us burning out quickly and filling ourselves with resentment for doing stuff for other people and not giving ourselves enough attention and love. However, giving your helping hand when it is asked for or needed also fills your heart with happiness. Balance your self-care with the joy that you feel helping your loved ones or even strangers that step into your life. It's all about digging into your feelings and rejoicing in happiness with whatever you are doing in your life.

Overall Recap of Loving Yourself First

Now that we know self-love and self-worth are essential to our happiness, and we deserve every bit of it, how do we include it in our daily lives? The most important thing you need to do, to include this practice in your daily life, is to believe in yourself and loving yourself first. No one can or should do that for you. Stop feeling guilty for taking care of yourself. Be more mysterious with your words and actions! Stop telling people everything that is happening in your life. Let your actions represent who you are instead of your words. Respect your goals and your ideas by keeping them private, so you avoid people putting their nose in your business and getting involved in your life. You will avoid people's unwanted opinions, disapprovals, and jealousy when you respect your privacy. Beware of your boundaries and enforce them. Boundaries are made by individuals to protect themselves from hurt, uncomfortable situations, and unhappiness. Make sure you stick to your boundaries no matter how the other person reacts. Do not feel guilty or weak to break your boundaries for anyone. Protect who you are and what you believe in and what you stand for in life, by not allowing people to cross your redlines. Stop any self- limiting beliefs about yourself. The voice inside your head trying to drag you down has been built from past bad experiences, traumas, and negative talk from society. If you let that voice get to you, it will kill your dreams in life and make you doubt yourself. When you let self-doubt kill your dreams and ambitions, you will stay in your comfort zone without taking action to improve your life and let people take advantage of you. Saying positive affirmations to yourself and taking action in your life, especially when self-limiting beliefs occur in your mind, will help you to push forward with your dreams and goals and improve yourself. Do not seek permission or approval from anyone. We were created to be ourselves. We have the ability to think, live, and behave the way we feel makes us happy. We don't need anyone's approval or permission to seek happiness in our lives. Put yourself and your needs first. You will be happier and it will be easier to help others when you take care of yourself first. Rest and exercise should be a daily ritual to restore and energize your body, spirit, and mind. When you are running on low fuel from little to no rest, your mind will be foggy, and your motivation will decline. This can affect your success and your energy to keep moving forward proficiently. And lastly, remember, you're the only one who knows what your boundaries are, what you want, what makes you happy, and what your needs are. Don't assume anyone will know. It is your priority in life to find your happiness in your journey through life. Take care of yourself first, because no one else will know how to take care of you better than you!

Our Imperfections: Boundaries

"Every woman that finally figured out her worth has picked up her suitcases of pride and boarded a flight to freedom, which landed in the valley of change" – *Shannon L. Alder*

Rule # 1: In all your interactions with people, enforce your boundaries. Enforcing your boundaries is one of the major keys to a successful relationship with your spouse, friends, mother, cousin, or anyone you encounter. Your boundaries are what keep you safe and content with yourself and your relationships. However, many people struggle with enforcing their boundaries, which leads them to the sin of holding grudges, anger, feelings of resentment, and even hatred towards their relationships. You may notice within yourself, that you want to enforce your own boundaries more with people. Unfortunately, guilt, fear of hurting other people's feelings, and people-pleasing, may cause you to step over your boundaries. Proverbs 4:23 warns us, *"Above all things, guard your heart for it is the wellspring of life."* When the verse says, "above all things," that means you need to make guarding your heart top priority, because it is the "wellspring" or the "source" of life. If you don't make your heart happy and make it a top priority, life will not flow so easily for you. So, how do we guard our hearts above all things without hurting other people's feelings or disappointing them?

"When we fail to set boundaries and hold people accountable, we feel used and mistreated. This is why we sometimes attack who they are, which is far more hurtful than addressing a behavior of choice." -Brene Brown

Mistake # 1: Your friend calls you on a Friday night and asks you to babysit so she can get some work done. Your brain is racing through your thoughts and maybe saying to you, *"My friend is single and struggling with balancing work and her daughter. I really need to say yes, even though I was looking forward to this concert with my hubby tonight. We haven't been able to spend that much time together lately because of our work schedules."* You say yes to your friend, thinking you are being nice, doing her a favor. However, you feel resentment towards your friend on Friday night. You have her daughter watch a movie and go to bed early instead of play games with her like you normally would do. You wish you were with your hubby, at that concert, singing your lungs out. You did not guard your heart. You filled it with resentment towards your friend. You also did not make spending quality time with your hubby, the concert, or your own personal day off from work a top priority. Here is the million-dollar question: Why do you feel the need to suffer just because someone else is suffering? It is not your responsibility to hold people's suffering onto your shoulders, especially when you don't have your own life together. Your responsibility is taking care of yourself and making your heart as happy as possible. Boundaries are part of who you are, your self-worth, and your self-respect. Don't fear hurting other people's feelings, getting them angry, or losing their relationship when it comes to being firm with your boundaries. People are allowed to feel whatever they want to feel, even if that means they feel disappointed or upset with you sticking to your boundary. Guard your heart from people stepping over or insulting your boundaries. The more you let your relationships take advantage of you, the more resentful you will feel towards them, even if they are supposed to be your best friend or favorite family member. Many people want to find an easy way to solve their problems, make their loneliness go away, pick up their groceries for them... etc. The more you say yes, the more they will lean on you. When you enforce what works for you and what doesn't work for you, you show people that you value yourself. They will learn that they need to respect you and your boundaries more.

45

Mistake # 2: Another common mistake people tend to make is thinking they will be liked more if they say yes. Here's the thing, you do not want to base your self-worth on making people like you and accept you. You must find your self-worth in accepting yourself and what you want out of life. You will find through your experience in life, saying yes to everything, will not give you a golden star sticker or brownie points. The other person will just think you can handle more tasks and responsibility. They will take more advantage of you and use you up to do whatever they want. Yes, even loved ones will do this to you whether they realize it or not. You may think saying yes at work will make you look like a hard worker in front of your boss, even though you're overworked, and the work schedule is not really convenient for you. Yes, you may look like a hard worker in front of your boss, but what if the company no longer needs your position? Will they really care how hard you work, or would they worry more about doing what is best for the company, which is illuminating your position and possibly laying you off work? The pain and disappointment are not worth more than the time you could have spent with family and friends, instead of endlessly overworking, just to people-please. It is different when you say yes to someone, for your own benefit, like working extra hours at work, because you want to make some extra money for your vacation, instead of doing it for someone else like your coworkers or boss to make them happy. Learn the difference.

Mistake # 3: Another reason you may overstep your boundaries is for the sake of avoiding conflict. You would rather let the other person have their way than actually standing up for what you want in order to avoid upsetting the other person. Running away from confrontation is easier than getting uncomfortable and having an awkward talk. But this path will never make you happy, and your heart won't be satisfied. Get out of your comfort zone. Have the awkward talk, and stand up for yourself. Don't fear the reactions of others more than disappointing yourself.

Instead of building your heart with grudges, hurt, and resentment, guard your heart from pain, by being firm with your boundaries. Always put your needs first, so when it comes time for you to truly help others or let them have it their way, you do it happily, with your whole heart, rather than with a heavy one.

Stand Up for your Boundaries Gracefully

Keeping your boundaries firm in their place does involve being kind and honest when you communicate your boundaries to others. When you need to stand up for your wants and needs, avoid lashing out, defending yourself as if you are guilty, and avoid being rude. Learn to be graceful when communicating with other people your boundaries without causing an unpleasant situation. For example: Your shopping with your best friend and she constantly tries to force you to buy things that are not your style or out of your budget. You don't want to hurt her feelings about the fact that her style is not your thing. You are also embarrassed about your low budget situation. The next time she picks out something you don't like or is overpriced, you can communicate your boundary by saying, *"You are so sweet to care about what I buy and how I look. My shopping addiction has me on a tight budget right now, so I have to be very selective with the pieces I'm buying."* She may keep grabbing a few pieces to show you. All you have to do is give a big smile and say, *"Cute! It will look better on you!"* She will eventually get the point and stop. You can also be totally straight forward and tell her the truth, *"Girl, that is not my style!"*

Boundaries are very useful with the people we love. Let's say your mom is getting involved in personal matters you don't want her to get involved in. Instead of yelling at her and avoid talking to her, you would have a kind, truthful, and awkward conversation with her, about how you don't want anyone to get involved in your personal issues. You would rather make the decision on your own terms. She most likely just wants to help you, but no matter what her reaction is, guard your heart, and be

47

true to your feelings. Anyone may try to test your boundaries, even your own mom. If she tries to test you by opening the subject again, you can simply say in a kind matter, *"Okay mom, we already talked about how I don't want to talk about this, and I want to make my own choice. If you don't change the subject, I am going to have to hang up and call you tomorrow."* Firm, kind, and truthful.

What's So Funny?

Another way to handle your boundaries is by turning a situation into a humorous one. Humor is one of the loveliest ways to get through any situation. It breaks through embarrassment and awkwardness as well. You have to be pretty quick to think on your feet and be creative when a person wants to break your boundary, and you want to tell them no while making them laugh. Let's say you're inviting your friends over for a party. Your sister comes over to help you cook dinner. You start to set up the table with your fine china. Your sister scolds you and tries to persuade you not to use the china unless it's a very special occasion and to use paper plates instead. You were so excited to use your fine china, and she just popped your happy bubble. Instead of arguing back, you decide to communicate your boundary by making a joke. You tell her, *"So, basically you want me to wait to use them when the President decides to come over? No thanks, I want to enjoy them with the people I love, right now!"* Your clever comment or humor will usually be taken with a light heart. Most people don't argue with humor and think twice about what they have said. If you can turn a situation into a joke, then you truly have a gift that will spark people's interest in you and respect your boundaries quicker and with less personal offense taken.

Our Imperfections: Judgment

"Once you awaken you will have no interest in judging those who sleep." - Anonymous

There is a type of freedom you won't be able to experience until you learn how to truly let go of judgment of others and judgment of yourself. Judgment of others can be a source of negativity, insecurity, false accusations, gossip, and jealousy. Judging yourself comes from a lack of self-confidence, a lack of self-love, and focusing on your imperfections. As long as judgment is part of your heart, mind, and conversations, you won't be able to feel a sense of freedom, to live life to your fullest, without fear of others, and fear of failure. This may hurt you, and hold you back in your life. When you learn it's not your responsibility to judge others, you will live free. When you stop judging yourself, you start to chase your dreams and your goals more without fear. When you accept others judging you, you will feel sympathy towards them, and you will be able to let their judgment of you go without feeling threatened or believing that their judgment of you is real.

Live Free Without Judgment of Yourself and Others

Enjoy life's freedom by choosing not to judge yourself. Accept your boundaries, your beliefs, what foods you like, what clothes you like to wear, who your friends are, and how you choose to live your life Get comfortable with who you are and accept your authentic personality. This will give you a boost of self-confidence and self-love. When you love yourself, you are less likely to judge your mistakes and experiences in life. You will accept them as part of your journey. Accepting your imperfections and mistakes as a part of who you are, leads to a judgment-free zone. Your judgment-free zone about yourself will help you excel in whatever your heart desires in life. When you learn to be delicate with

49

yourself and your feelings, you are then able to do the same for others. Never judging others or yourself does not mean a judgment won't ever pass through your mind. It means that when you catch yourself judging, you sprinkle love on it to make your judgment disappear. If you find yourself judging your body, for instance, become aware of what you are saying and sprinkle love on top. As soon as the negative thought starts flowing, stop it by appreciating all the hard work your body is doing for you. When it comes to judging others, a great technique to use is to act like their older sibling by defending them. You got cut in line at the grocery store. Instead of judging that person as rude and unforgivable, be their "older sibling" and defend them. Maybe they need to run home to their sick child and weren't paying attention. Maybe this person was actually being rude, and having a really horrible day. Try to be positive and see the better side of situations. Especially, situations that really have no meaning to us and we are better off letting go than hanging on to their negative energy. You don't know what people are going through or thinking. Avoid assuming people's thinking and actions as well. That's part of judging. *"Everyone has untold stories of pain and sadness that make them love and live a little different than you do. Stop judging. Instead, try to understand."* -Anonymous

Our Imperfections: Pain

"All suffering is caused by ignorance. People inflict pain on others in the selfish pursuit of their own happiness or satisfaction." – Dalai Lama

How many times have you encountered painful comments, unnecessary jabs, and hurtful actions? *"Why did my girlfriends go out to sushi without me, even though they know I have the night off? Why did mom embarrass me in front of the family like that? Why did my coworker throw me under the bus...? Didn't I just do a big favor for her last week? Why did my aunt make that rude comment? Why did my best friend betray me? Why would my husband say something like that to me?"*

As imperfect humans living in this imperfect world, we are surrounded by misunderstandings, miscommunication, and pain. We are also surrounded by other people's pain as well as our own that we have experienced in our lives. You need to know that associating yourself with other people means you are opening yourself to receive their wounds and bad experiences in their life, and mixing it with your own. This is part of communication with people that cannot be avoided. However, you can learn how to deal with it so that you can protect your happiness bubble.

Work Within

One of the most important things for you to do, to protect yourself from pain that might be inflicted from others, is by working within yourself. You need to become aware of your own wounds that you have developed throughout your life. When someone makes a comment about your height, do you feel pain because you were made fun of when you were younger at school for being short? Do you always have to explain in detail why you make certain decisions in your life because you didn't grow up with anyone teaching you to trust your own decisions? When your close friend didn't invite you to her big party, do you feel left out, like when no one wanted to hang out with you at recess? These can be hurtful situations you may encounter with family, friends, and strangers. That's why it's important to build your self-confidence within yourself. Learn to love who you are. Accept what other people think and say to you without taking it personally and reacting. When you are faced with someone inflicting pain on you, like a hurtful comment, imagine the painful comment as if it was a thunderstorm. Watch the storm out the window and wait for it to pass by without reacting to it. Stay calm and move on with your life again once it passes. You will drive people crazy when they see that they could not get a reaction out of you. They want you to react and fall down; however, it's very important in these times to not even let them think whatever they did or said even mattered to you. And honestly, it shouldn't! Keep in mind to work on healing your wounds and pain from the past. When you work within, you will be able to smile and not be bothered by your girlfriends when they go out for sushi without inviting you.

It's Not You… It's Them

When you are communicating with people, it's so important to keep in mind that they have wounds and pain that you may or may not know of, just like you do.

Rude comments and not so nice actions have to do with them and how they are feeling. When you dig deeper into their hurtful actions towards you, usually you will find the person was insecure or jealous, or the same thing was said about them or done to them before, and they want to pass the pain down to another person. When people don't treat us nicely, our first instinct is to defend ourselves. But how many times can you recall defending yourself actually to work in these situations? Notice that when you defend yourself, people will either argue with you or interrupt you while you're talking and totally ignore what you are saying.

They don't want to hear your side of the story. They want to believe whatever they want about you and make you feel uncomfortable for whatever reason. This is the time to smile, change the subject, and focus the conversation back on them and their life. Remember, it's all about them and nothing about you.

Here's another food for thought: When you start to improve yourself, some people are going to look up to you and be inspired by you. Unfortunately, others will feel threatened, become toxic, and try to drag you down. They may even be loved ones you never expected to become negative towards you. Let go of these people and invite them back into your life when they are ready for the new you.

"Happiness is a choice, not a result. Nothing will make you happy until you choose to be happy. No person will make you happy unless you decide to be happy. Your happiness will not come to you. It can only come from you." – Ralph Marston

Run!

When all else fails with toxic people, just run! Run from any family, any friends, coworkers, or anyone you encounter from your life that is full of negativity and drama. It's okay to let people go who put a heavy weight on your life. It's okay to not call back that person who makes knots in your stomach. It's okay to leave a party that is turning into a drama event. It's okay to excuse yourself from a conversation that is full of gossip. And if people are crossing your boundaries with their toxic behavior, don't be shy to tell people who are crossing your boundary that their behavior is not acceptable. Just remember, people's negative reactions towards you, is really about them, and their insecurities and life struggles. Send love towards them. Be understanding. You don't need to defend yourself. Show who you really are through your actions. And if you really need to, run away!

Practice in Your Daily Life

1. Learn to forgive yourself for any past mistakes. Forgive others for hurting you as well.
2. Work on being confident in the way you look and how you live your life, and in the choices you make.
3. Learn to smile at a mean comment instead of throwing one back at the person. (They are already in pain, or they wouldn't have said it.)
4. Forgiveness is very important for being able to let go. But that doesn't mean you let people walk over your boundaries.
5. Avoid judging others, and replace your judgment with a positive outlook.
6. Avoid judging yourself.
7. Change a judgment you make by turning it into a more positive statement.
8. Stick to your boundaries.
9. Stay away from jealousy, drama, and gossip.

Enhance Your Life

(even with daily struggles)

"Even now as broken as you may feel you are still so strong. There's something to be said for how you hold yourself together and keep moving even though you feel like shattering. Don't stop. This is your healing. It doesn't have to be pretty or graceful. You just have to keep going." -Maxwell Diawuoh

This chapter talks about different topics that may hold you back from becoming the woman you want to become. Practicing to take life one step at a time and learning how to get through your struggles while trying to stay positive, will help you enhance your life to the fullest.

Weight of the World

You're having your fruit yogurt and coffee in the morning in front of the TV before you start getting ready for the day. Your watching the news channel and get sucked into watching what's going on in the world. Another shooting in the city. A fatal car accident on the highway. A segment on how pollution is getting worse around the world. You sit on your couch with a knot in your stomach and a heavy weight that has come upon your shoulders. You ask yourself, what can you do to help this world become a better place? How can you make the problems in the world go away?

When you put the weight of the world on your delicate body, you are doing nothing good for yourself. It's not your job to solve all the problems of the world. You are not even capable of solving all the problems we see on TV and social media. Lift that burden from your shoulder and stop feeling guilty for not being able to solve all global problems. However, you can still do your part to make the world a better place by paying attention to how you are

55

contributing to the world. Are you aware of the unnecessary waste you make in your home? Do you try your best to recycle or limit any unnecessary electricity and water usage? Do you try your best to volunteer when you can or give out a helping hand to someone who needs it? Would you stop your busy day to help an injured animal on the side of the street? Do you support animal rights or human rights when situations face you? You don't have to go out looking for ways to make the world better if you are physically and emotionally unable to. Situations will present themselves in your personal life. You must do your best to help and improve these situations when you are able to. You are not expected to fight all the battles except the ones you are personally faced with and are able to fight. The most important thing you can do for this world is to spread your positive, vibrant energy to your home, your community, and where ever you go. Your energy by itself can do wonders for the negativity going around. Each person who is not feeding into the negative aspects of the world is enough.

Tip 1: Don't listen to the news. If there is something really important happening, you will hear from it in other ways, like talking to people or social media. Limit your negative exposures.

Tip 2: Instead of focusing on negative atmospheres that bring you down, focus your attention on the beauty of the world (mountains, beaches, romantic cities, beautiful islands, etc.)

Tip 3: Believing in a higher power and having faith in God and His love and protection for us will definitely help you lift your worry of the world.

Change your mind Change your Life

If you are unhappy with your job, your body, your relationship, your house, or whatever your unhappy situation is, then change it! There is no excuse for you to tolerate an unhappy situation. You are allowed to do whatever you put your mind to. Yes, it may be difficult, and you may have to work hard and make some sacrifices, but your goal is to keep and maintain your happiness throughout your life. If you decide you cannot change your circumstance for whatever reason, you must accept your situation and find reasons why your situation is a blessing. Find joy and gratitude in whatever you cannot change in your life. Let's say at this point in your life you are not happy with your weight. You would like to lose a few pounds and tone up. But for whatever reason, you are unable to. Instead of giving up and wearing baggy clothes to hide your figure, look for ways to enhance your figure. Accept the way you look and search for clothes to enhance your body. You can always find the style that looks good on your body and colors that accentuate the way you look. Enhance your favorite parts of your body. If you love your hair, focus on doing hairstyles every day to make you feel good. Until you are ready to work on perfecting your body the way you want. Don't give up on what you already have. It's your choice you have the two options in front of you. Get out of your comfort zone and start working harder to get the life you want or stop complaining about your life that you don't want to change. This is your life; don't let fear or others choose happiness for you. You choose your adventure. Go out and pursue your happiness and leave excuses and fear behind.

Breaking the Negative Cycle

You stayed up watching Netflix Sunday night, and you missed your last snooze button in the morning. Now you're running really late for class. You get to your class and realize you misunderstood the due date of a project you had to do that ended up being due today, not next Monday. Your whole day feels ruined. It may even ruin your entire week. Thoughts like *"Why does this happen to me?"* or *"I've been cursed"* run through your brain. Your energy and thoughts towards your obstacles, fears, mistakes, and unpleasant situations are going to *"make you or break you"* What if you were able to view your unpleasant life situations without drama, guilt, fear, sadness, and anger. Our human

57

experiences will come with imperfection and obstacles. Accept that you can't avoid failure, bad experiences, and unpleasant situations. Our imperfect life is what keeps us growing, learning and improving ourselves. Don't keep viewing your imperfect life as a bad life, bad luck, or cursed.

Handle Your Negative Situations

Let's go back to your morning. You may feel ashamed, worried, or anxious at the moment. These are common feelings that will either escalate or die down, depending on how you talk to yourself. Your worry and irritation will continue throughout the day if you keep negative thoughts rolling in your mind causing yourself other problems. But if you take responsibility for any situation thrown at you and turn it to a positive matter, you will succeed far more in your life. Skip the drama you cause yourself and believe that there is a lesson and even good that comes out of any situation. Your bad morning has offered you the chance to rethink your morning routine and organize your life better. Waking up earlier, using daily planners, setting reminders for the next day will help you have a better morning. Even if you do have a positive attitude and some other obstacles pop up during the day, like forgetting to pick up celery after coming home from the grocery store to make the soup you planned for dinner; don't give up your positive attitude. Keep going to succeed and grow. You will be put in situations that are worse than others like a death of a loved one. It's okay to feel your sadness, pain, and anxiety. However, don't keep dwelling on those negative feelings. Keep going and find the light that your situation is hiding. If you get sick with the flu, learn to appreciate your good health and take care of yourself better. If you lose your job, let the opportunity lead you to your dream job. If you fail a test, learn the material again and discover new information you didn't pay attention to before. Applaud yourself for finding a way out of a situation and solving any problems that come your way with calmness, patience, and an open mind to keep doing better.

58

The Simple Life: Money

(Part 1)

Money and stress go hand in hand for many of us living in today's society. Whether we make a six-figure salary or minimum wage, plenty of people are in debt, living paycheck to paycheck and trying to find ways to make more money to make ends meet. Many of us are missing the main problem causing all of this money stress. It's not really about how much people are making. It's more about people not living within their means. People want to keep up with the luxurious materialistic lifestyles they see. They think shopping will make them happy, or owning more will keep them safe and satisfied. They are not aware of how much they are spending. It's been seen over and over again that the more money society makes, the more they spend and upgrade their life. Making more money is not really solving problems. Taking control of our financial situation and budgeting is what will really bring financial happiness and freedom.

Take Advantage of Your Hard-Earned Money

Since we have the luxury of easily accessing anything we need or want, we have lost control of our bad habits that put us in financial troubles. We forget to appreciate everything we own and use it up to its fullest potential and pollute the world with the waste we don't use or need. We also forget that a simple life, including a simple abundance of materials leads to a happy fulfilled life. We forget that we don't need to slave at work to buy a luxury car. We just need a car to get us from point A to point B. We forget to value what we own because it is so easy to just buy another one. It's now the new normal to have a collection of stuff and fill up our house, so there's not a single space that's empty. We live in a time where eating out every day is a part of our life

59

because we are too busy, too tired, and too lazy to cook at home. This fast world of food, fashion, cars, and life, in general, is creating an enormous amount of stress, fatigue, and anxiety. The funny part is, media makes it look like the faster we go with easy access to drive-thrus and easy next day deliveries, the easier our life gets. We are having difficulty as a society, slowing down and enjoying life the way we should be.

Taking It All for Granted

You may feel accomplished going through the newspaper weekly to find coupons and ways to save your hard-earned money while still buying what you need. You may miss the real joy of searching for the perfect lipstick to splurge on as a reward for passing an important exam. You may miss the excitement of waiting for a special occasion for your husband to take you to a fancy dinner that you look forward to. There is nothing wrong with enjoying splurges and luxuries in life. These are gifts for us to enjoy. However, the problem hits when we take advantage of these luxuries, especially if we are using them daily or weekly and take them for granted. What we use to look at as rewards and luxuries, has just become another handbag you stuff in your closet or another restaurant you dined at. Taking these things for granted takes away the excitement of making that handbag a special occasion you have been planning to get yourself. Eating out at a fine restaurant with a beautiful view becomes another restaurant that you're sitting in, scrolling through emails and texts instead of enjoying the scenery. If we have the luxury to buy what we want but stop appreciating what we have and take them for granted, where's the happiness in that?

Money Stress

Money can truly be a stressor and a very sensitive subject to many people if not appreciated and used correctly. Illuminating money issues can rule out a tough life, anxiety, and depression.

When there are money issues, it can be a major source of unhappiness in people's lives. Unfortunately, it's something people tend to ignore and avoid dealing with. But you can't put money issues on the back burner and hope it goes away. You must face the truth about your bank account, personal money struggles, solve any money problems, and create future money goals for yourself. Get to the level in your life of being proud of having everything under control and working in achieving your goals. If you're thinking of your financial situation and it is not ideal, don't worry or panic. Whatever situation you are in is where you are supposed to be in your life. You can learn from your past mistakes and improve yourself for the future. Embrace your financial situation and any other life situation and better yourself every day.

Money Solutions

To be able to improve your financial status, it's important to be aware of your financial situation. Ask yourself questions like, *why are you in the situation you are in now? Do you use shopping as emotional therapy? Are you eating out all the time, instead of investing in your health? Are you trying to keep up with the Joneses? Do you have negative emotions towards money? Do you believe there is a hole in your wallet? Are you carrying along bad money habits you learned from your parents?* These are all common money situations that may come up. However, it is your job to reverse whatever bad habit you need to work on.

Reverse Your Feelings

Illuminating any fear you have towards money is the first thing you need to do. Money is not bad. Money is good and buys us nice things. Money lets us take vacations, and fills us up when we are hungry. Money keeps us safe and puts a roof over our heads. Don't listen to anyone who tells you money is bad or evil. You can do bad and evil things with money, but that doesn't mean it is evil.

Another thing you need to do is avoid talking bad about money. When your friends are sitting at the bar on a Friday night talking about how broke they are, or if you're shopping with your girlfriend and she complains to you how she doesn't have enough to buy the things she wants. Ignore the complaints. Do not engage in these types of negative conversations about money. The more you complain about money, the less you will have of it. When you have a bad thought about money, replace the thought with something positive. Do not fear it. There is an abundance of it to go around for anyone who wants it. It is here to help us live our best lives.

Appreciating Money

Look at your bank account when your paycheck is deposited and say thank you! Thank the money you have for being there. Appreciate what it does for you. Appreciate that it buys you gas to go places and restaurants to eat and enjoy your time out. When you appreciate, more will be attracted to you.

Respecting Money

Respecting your money has a lot to do with how you spend your money. If you spend your money mindlessly, you are disrespecting your money. Your money has been earned from hard work that you put time and effort into making. Don't waste it on things you don't need or use. And avoid buying excessive amounts of things like food that gets thrown away because it doesn't get used up in time.

Keeping Up with the Joneses

There's absolutely nothing wrong with owning pretty luminous high-end things. You are well worth the glam and luxury. However, when you purchase beautiful and expensive items on credit cards, leaving you in debt just to keep up with the Joneses, that's when you really feel the pain. Instead of enjoying your luxury life, you spend it biting your nails trying to figure out how you are going to pay off your credit cards while still living paycheck to paycheck. This unnecessary stress in your life is created to keep up with the Joneses. And whoever you're trying to keep up with, there's a good chance they are trying to keep up with you or someone else. Live your life at the level you are able to. If you want more, work harder at receiving more. Be content and happy with what you receive in life, and don't take advantage of it. People-pleasing your parents, cousins, friends, boss, strangers, and even your haters are not worth the financial headache. There's also no value in not being true to yourself and your lifestyle situation.

Save It

Do you have a savings account that you could live off of for a year? Most people don't. Statistics in America say that 70% of people live paycheck to paycheck. Basically, if they have an emergency or lose their jobs, their life hits a fan. Having extra cash saved will make you feel safe and secure in your life. You won't feel like you're living off of the cliff of a mountain. It takes time, patience, consistency, and motivation off the couch to save money. Even if you're in debt, it's highly recommended to save a little cash for an emergency, so you don't have to put that emergency on top of your old debt.

Encouraging Tips to Financial Freedom

There's plenty of different ways to organize your savings and spending. The easiest way is to cut your spending and illuminate things you can survive without for a while. Another way is to get an extra job even if it's just temporary. Budgeting, talking to financial advisors, and organizing your bills are very successful ways to deal with any money issues. Anxiety will lessen once you have more control over your finances. Take an afternoon with some tea or even a glass of wine to write down all your bills.

Figure out what your weaknesses are when it comes to making a hole in your wallet. You could do some side hustles temporarily to pay off debt or save more money. However, most of the time, all it takes is some budgeting, downsizing, and patience. You may also need to isolate yourself from certain people in your life temporarily or permanently who disturb your new lifestyle and goals. You can make budgeting fun by challenging yourself and creating a game out of it. It will take preparation, research, trial and error, and dedication on your part just like a healthy weight loss journey. Don't forget to appreciate, respect, save, and look at money through a new lens. Face your money fears, start saving and pay off your debt and take control of your finances so you can live happy and feel safe in your life. It's your money, your life, and your happiness.

The Simple Life: Life at Its Simplest (part 2)

"The goal of minimalism is not just to own less stuff. The goal is to unburden our lives, so we can accomplish more." -Joshua Becker

The world has become overly busy, overly complicated, and too scheduled. Stress and anxiety are our new norm. Society is always competing with the best new thing. A better body, a better car, a better house, more hours at work to make more money, more parties, more activities, more, more, and more. Society not only encourages us to compete with each other, but it actually applauds the life of bigger, better, and more. People don't even know how to live stress-free and simple anymore. Deep down inside of us, we would love to just relax and live a simpler life. However, the simple life is not impressive in today's lifestyle. Mothers will be gathered in the park talking with one another about how much they do during the day and how many activities their kids are involved in. It's a competition. You rarely hear people talking about sleeping early to get their rest or having a relaxing day with no long to-do list to take care of. Not many people realize that this competitive lifestyle is part of our unhappiness, anxiety, and stress. The high-stress level of our daily lives is making us sick and develop all kinds of diseases. So, in this complex world, how do we slow down and simplify our lives for the sake of maintaining our good health and happiness?

The Right Type of Abundance

"Like the air you breathe, abundance in all things is available to you. Your life will simply be as good as you allow it to be." – Abraham Hicks

Before talking about simplifying your life, it's important to shed light on the topic of fulfilling your life with abundance. While you're on the journey to simplicity, keep in mind to practice abundance in what you love for the sake of your happiness.

My own experience with abundance:

When I first learned about minimalism, I jumped on board and hoped this was the answer to my prayers for materialistic freedom. I researched minimalism through endless blogs, YouTube videos, and Netflix documentaries. I started cleaning out my closet, makeup, bathroom, kitchen, books, and other categories in my life I could downsize. It felt amazing to open any door in my house and see a clean and empty space. I loved the feeling of picking out my favorite lipstick to wear without rummaging through a drawer full of lipsticks I never even touched. I was on my way to living the simple life. However, shortly after the decluttering and purging of my things, I would get a feeling of anxiety and overwhelming feeling since I felt a lack of materials in my life. I just felt like I didn't have enough things anymore for my comfort. I would worry that I would run out of shampoo, or my dogs would eat my only pair of leggings I own. So, the cycle started all over again, and I found myself buying things again. My life was filled with materialistic things that I would end up decluttering not long after purchasing them. I didn't understand what was going on. Why did it feel good to declutter my life and only own what I need and love but at the same time felt anxious with my lack of materials? I finally learned what would solve my problem. I learned how important it is to have abundance in what you need and love. It is true that we should limit our items that we own to live a simpler life and only bring what we love into our lives. But how much better is it to bring what we love into our lives with abundance? Some people may be okay with living with just enough. However, many people like myself will find comfort in living a lifestyle with abundance. My minimalist journey did help me understand what I love, what looks good on me, and what works for me. I cleared everything else in my life. The next part I had to work on was relieving any anxiety I was feeling from not having enough. I started to buy and store multiples of what I love in my closets and drawers. If I loved a certain shampoo, I would buy more than one at a time. I would stalk up on even more when there was a sale on an item I want. I also started doing this with my pantry, as well. Instead of running out to the store when I need an ingredient, I would buy a few of what I use often. Keeping my pantry stalked brought me comfort, knowing I have what I need and more. Living in abundance with what you need and love will bring you comfort. It is important to feel satisfied instead of always feeling like your body and mind are not satisfied. Just be aware of the type of abundance you fill your life with.

Declutter Your Life

More and more people are realizing the benefits of decluttering and living a minimalist lifestyle. The minimalist movement has changed the way people live dramatically. Minimalists are downsizing their houses, belongings, and to-do lists to live more simply. People are self-disciplining themselves to live a simpler life by using strategies like the 33-item wardrobe, project pan, and the no spending year. You can find countless people sharing their journey on YouTube, blog posts, and other types of social media. This lifestyle is going against the materialistic world we live in. However, it is possible to discipline yourself to only use what you have, save money for important goals, and illuminate any shopaholic habits. When you decide you want to declutter your materialistic life, you will open doors for yourself and not feel trapped and overwhelmed by clutter, debt, and possessions. When starting the declutter journey, review constantly things you don't want or need. Get rid of anything that does not stand for who you are or make you happy. Do you own ripped clothes or mismatched pajamas? Get rid of them. Represent yourself in a high-value way even when you are the only one in the house seeing yourself. Do you keep extra cooking ingredients just in case you ever feel like pulling out your chef hat? Pass the items to someone who will actually use them and appreciate owning them. You won't have to rummage through these unused items to get to what you actually need and use anymore. Know what you have and get familiar with your stuff, so you don't accidentally buy yourself another one because you didn't realize you already own it. Only keep items you are using that fit in with your lifestyle. Don't keep anything you wish would fit in with your lifestyle, but realistically doesn't work for you, like those expensive high-end shoes you thought you could do your grocery shopping in every day, just like the Instagram girls. Declutter every aspect of your life. Declutter your closet, kitchen, fridge, books, phone, even people in your life. One of the harder things to remove from your life is sentimental items. Things like a gift from a special someone in your life that's taking up space and puts an overwhelming feeling over you needs to be decluttered. As long as you're not using the gift and it brings no value to your life, don't feel guilty giving it away to someone who may use it. Keeping a gift does not represent your relationship with that person. It only represents a loving gesture from them telling you, "I thought of you" It has nothing to do with the item gifted. After you are done decluttering all the areas of your life, congratulate yourself and do it again! Don't forget decluttering is a continuous process, not a onetime thing. We are constantly bringing items into our lives, and we need to frequently check what we own and declutter what we don't need.

Simplify and Save

Social media has a big influence on your paycheck. Advertisements around us are launching new products constantly. Companies and brands have used their intelligence to use social media influencers to advertise all the new products being created. They contact social media influencers to advertise and sell whatever these companies are launching to get everyone more interested in buying and trying out their products. It's a wonderful and easy way for people to learn about products and items that will be useful for them. However, purchasing things that are being advertised has gotten out of control. For example, if you found a face cleanser you love and already works with your budget and skin, then why would you own hundreds of face cleansers you don't even know you have? You have one face. You don't need ten other face cleansers to wash your face. This is a growing spending problem for many women getting sucked in by social media to buy everything that's on sale and being advertised. Don't let media fool you into purchasing a bunch of things you don't need just because it's the new "best thing." They want you to spend money so they can make money. And they advertise in a way to make you think you need it and want it and you gotta have it. Since there are countless different companies and products, research well what you spend your money on. If you find products, you already love, try to stick to them and be thankful you found what you love and what works for you. Simplify your makeup and skincare products to what you love. Simplify your closet as well. Wear what works for you and what compliments your body. Be aware of all the pictures you scroll through on your phone of pretty girls wearing pretty styles. Become familiar with what clothing fits well with your body, so you don't get sucked into buying clothes that don't fit your body or lifestyle. Avoid shopping with friends who pressure you into buying things you know will end up in the back of your drawers. When you do decide to purchase things, buy within your means, and avoid overspending. Purchase what you love and what makes you feel fabulous. If you make a purchase mistake, don't feel guilty. Find it a new home and learn from your experience.

Simplify your To-Do List

Aside from simplifying your material possessions, you can probably agree that you also need to work on simplifying your to-do list and activities taking up too much time in your life. Ask yourself, what can you get rid of in your life? Are you overbooking your day with too many errands and activities? Try to pick 2-3 priorities from your to-do list to get done every day. If you get any additional things done, consider it an added bonus. If you only are able to get these 2-3 tasks done, enjoy the accomplishment of getting your necessities done each day. Keep your activities simple and limited. One or two activities you can put your time and energy on a week is more productive than timelessly running from one activity to the next. Your activities and hobbies may change after a while, and you can move on to whatever makes you happy at the moment. You may feel out of place at first when you learn to be easy on yourself and not overbook your day and feel guilty for not finishing your long list of to-dos. However, you will find your days much more productive and giving more energy and effort in whatever you choose to do that day.

Learning the Magic Word, No

The more we say yes to things we don't want to do, the more we put our wants and needs on the back burner. The more we let other people's comments and opinions influence us, the less we believe in ourselves, and the less we put our happiness as a priority. You need to believe that your happiness is worth coming first. Practice saying no to a party when you would rather relax at home and sleep early. Practice saying no to your boss for putting in overtime at work when you want to spend time with your family. Practice skipping doing an inconvenient favor for a friend when you have your own errands to get done. The people who love you will understand. You may have noticed in your own life if you are a "yes" person that you don't really earn many brownie points or rewards for stepping over your happiness for others. You may have even experienced people taking more advantage of you when you people please, and not many favors are returned to you. Learn to respect your time and respect your life. It's important to practice saying no because it won't always come naturally and easily. It may even be difficult sometimes or uncomfortable to say no. But your level of relief and happiness will improve dramatically.

70

Simplicity in your Home

How do you feel about cooking, cleaning, organizing, and folding? Is it an inconvenience? Do you find it boring or a waste of time? You may love to clean and cook on certain days. Other days, you may feel lazy or not in the mood to keep up with your housework. If you learn to enjoy homemaking, whether it's your home, apartment, or your bedroom, there is a certain peace and connection you will make when you are home.

You may love to eat out at restaurants all the time and come back to a clean and polished home after the housekeepers leave. These are wonderful blessings that we are able to enjoy that keep us stress-free and may simplify our schedules when we don't have to put cooking, cleaning, and ironing on our to-do list. However, learning to enjoy homemaking is something each of us should experience. Cooking, cleaning, and keeping your house organized and tidy can actually be therapeutic to your body and soul. We are a creation. You have the freedom to create and design in your own home however you please. You have the freedom to create through baking and mopping the floors without you probably realizing it. You decide whether to create a quick healthy meal in less than thirty minutes or if you want to make an exotic dish that takes a few hours of your time. You can clean in a quiet environment and listen to mother nature singing outside your window or play a podcast or audible book to keep you company. Homemaking can even be shared with others in your life. You can choose to clean out your closet or bake a cake with a sister or friend. It's the way you look at homemaking that brings happiness and peace into your home. There's also no better way to connect with your living space and appreciate the shelter and privacy it gives you than getting involved in your living space and taking the time to take care of it yourself.

Daily Routine

When you create a daily routine, you will feel safe and secure in your life. You know what to do from the moment you get out of bed to the time you go back to bed. Your routines should include daily healthy habits for your body and mind. They are made to guide you on the decisions you make throughout the day. Routines bring balance into your life. It's important to understand that you don't need to follow your routine every day. You may have an appointment in the morning. You might even wake up late one day. Many things may interrupt your daily routine. Life is also fun when there is some unexpected excitement or change of plans. Accept the fact that routines may change due to life events. However, if you feel lost or out of place during your day, you can always fall back on your routine to get through your day. They are created to keep you organized and goal-oriented. The purpose of them is to guide you through your daily tasks and everyday life, so you don't feel overwhelmed and waste time figuring out what to do next. You always have the freedom to change your routine through different phases of your life. Don't be afraid to change your routine to fit your lifestyle. Changing your routine means you're evolving and growing. You also may have different types of routines. You may also have a different daily routine for each day of the week. When you know when to exercise or pick up the groceries, you create repetitive tasks for yourself that will build simplicity in your life.

"When you do something beautiful and nobody noticed do not be sad. For the sun every morning is a beautiful spectacle and yet most of the audience still sleeps" - John Lennon

Morning Routine

Your morning has the power to make up the rest of your day. One of the most difficult habits for a person to succeed in a morning routine is waking up early. There are two simple tricks that you need to follow to make the process of waking up earlier, and easier. Sleep earlier. There is no way around it! Your body needs to be well-rested to start your day right. The other trick is to have a rewards system going for you in the morning. If waking up to exercise right away gets you up, that's great! Not everyone is able to wake up and look forward to exercise in the morning. You might be more interested to get out of bed, make yourself a warm cup of coffee, play a motivational podcast in the background while you take that time in the AM to get your hair and makeup done. You may be more interested in some "me" time and self-care in the morning that will help you start your day better and get you jumping out of bed. Not everyone can start being productive as soon as they get out of bed which is totally fine. Take it slow in the morning. It's up to you to find what will get you to stop hitting the snooze button and starting your day. Is it sitting in bed reading a book? Do you like to make a tasty, well thought out breakfast to enjoy with the family? Do you like to take your dog on a walk in the fall and watch the leaves change color? Do you like to book a manicure early in the morning to pamper yourself first thing in the AM, so you feel beautiful the rest of the day? Whatever it is that excites you, enjoy your morning and take time doing what you love. Your day will run smoother with a more relaxed you!

"She woke up every morning with the option of being anyone she wished. How beautiful it was that she always chose herself" – Tyler Kent White

You have to find what's your purpose of getting up in the morning. What will your routine be? When you get a routine down, your body will adapt to it. Most importantly, if you live with others, get up early enough so no one will distract you. Your mornings are a chance for you to wake up and start your day happy. When you are in the process of following a morning routine, do not feel like you failed if you keep hitting the snooze button. You may have to tweak it from time to time to fit your lifestyle. The ultimate goal of a morning routine is to wake up happy with a purpose, looking forward to the day. It does not necessarily have to be about being productive as soon as you wake up and burn out the rest of the day. Give yourself the opportunity to improve your day just by improving your morning. Make it all about you and how you want to set the mood for the day.

"Wake up my heart I will wake the dawn with my song" – *Psalm 57:8*

Night Routine

"Day is over, night has come. Today is gone, what's done is done. Embrace your dreams through the night. Tomorrow comes with a whole new light" – *George Orwell*

As the sun sets and darkness overcomes the sky, there's a certain peaceful and calming energy that arises with the mood. Just like the sun rises to tell us to wake up and start the day, the moon tells us to wind down and get ready to rest. Many people find that the best way to wind down after a long day is to eat dinner in front of the TV until it's time to sleep. This is definitely a relaxing and laid-back routine before bed, but is it the best night routine you can give yourself? Shutting off your brain at night may feel great; however, it's not the most productive and useful way to use your time at night. It's also not very productive to tirelessly rush finishing your to-do list, when you can just save your tasks for the next day when you have more energy. Your nighttime routine should consist of some fun preparation for the next day and finding closure for the day. Instead of your daily night time binge-watching TV shows, use your evening to do other things. Call a friend and meet at a coffee shop. Enjoy a fun family night event. Book a spa appointment before heading home from work. Go to a dance class at the gym. Winding down at night does not mean shutting off your brain completely. It means slowing down because the day is coming to an end for you to rest

74

and get ready for the next day to come. An hour before you sleep, find a short and simple routine that helps you prepare for the next day. This could be preparing lunch, packing your bag, or picking out your outfit for the next day. Try to get into a habit of washing your face, putting on a moisturizer, combing your hair, and brushing your teeth before bed. When you wash away the day and end it fresh, this will symbolize for you it's time to relax and sleep. The most important thing you can do for yourself right before you shut your eyes and sleep is to bring closure to your day. Bringing closure to your day means replaying the things you are grateful for that happened during the day. Another way to bring closure to your day is by meditating or praying and casting all your worries on God, which will help you fall asleep faster and easier. There is a certain type of contentment that overcomes your body, and you are able to release anxiety when you communicate with the high power any troubles you are facing. All in all, keep your lights dimmed and wash away your day. Wind down. Thank your stars. Say your prayers, and have a great night!

Single and Happy

"Single is not a status. It is a word that best describes a person who is strong enough to live and enjoy life without depending on others"
– Unknown

The most important relationship you need to focus on before anyone else is with yourself. You are the only person that truly understands what you like, what you don't like, what you need, and what you want. When you learn to be confident and always be there for yourself, you don't need anyone's opinions or approval to make you feel content. Being alone teaches you to make yourself happy first. Everyone else who is a part of your life is there to share happiness with you. So how do we become more comfortable being alone? What is so special about making ourselves happy first? What does being alone teach us when we are in relationships with others?

"Cinderella never asked for a prince. She asked for a night off with a dress." – Kierra Cass

Did you ever hear the phrase "You'll find your soulmate when you least expect it." Whoever you heard it from was right. When you're busy being alone and happy, everyone will find you attractive. People crave to have happy and confident people involved in their life. They want to be a part of that vibe. That's why you won't necessarily be truly alone when you learn to be happy while being single. Everyone wants to live with you in your happy bubble because not everyone can reach the potential of being so comfortable and happy being alone. As you grow during your single life and learn to be comfortable and happy being by yourself, you become more ready to meet your life partner. But, if you are looking for happiness and believe you will be happy only when you are in a relationship, you will most likely fail at happiness. When you find the right person to go through life with, they should only be adding more happiness to your life, not be the source of your happiness. It's not your partner's job to fill up your happiness tank. Nobody wants that kind of responsibility anyways, not even you in your relationships. It's difficult to be a person's source of happiness and its energy draining. Imagine that your mom, sister, or best friend has to rely on you all the time to make them happy. They may expect you to take them out everywhere, always be there for them when they need you, spend all your free time with them, and vent to you about everything and anything. That is definitely energy draining. Men feel the same way. They don't want you to rely on them for your happiness. Men looking for a relationship are interested in a confident and happy woman who is comfortable being who she is and showing ambition about her life. That's the attraction men are looking for. So, make sure when you are out and about, you dress up and have fun with only the intention of enjoying yourself and celebrating your life. Mr. Right will be watching out for you.

The Happy and Single Life

Being alone teaches you to trust yourself. It teaches you to not care about others opinions of how you should live your life. It lets you work on your dreams and goals with no interruptions. It helps you discover why you want to roll out of bed in the morning and embrace life. The whole point of you learning to be comfortable by yourself is so you won't rely on anyone else to make you happy. This way, when you are in a relationship, you are not trying to find yourself and who you are within the relationship. This also prepares you for when you do meet that special someone; you know exactly who you are and what you want out of the relationship and life in general. Your self-confidence will be very attractive to the right man. He doesn't have any pressure that your happiness relies on him, and you don't make him feel like it's his job to make you happy. He knows you can make yourself happy with or without him. Being single and happy not only gives you an idea of who you want to be in your relationship, but it also will give you a clearer view of whether any relationship you are in is right for you or you need to push the next button.

Here's the thing you also need to understand. It's okay to be single and enjoy life, but at the same time, feel loneliness, or that you wish you had a relationship. These emotions may naturally come up from time to time. There is nothing wrong with wanting a partner to spend the rest of your time with. But, it's not okay to obsess over finding a man, making it a top priority on your to-do list, and forgetting about enjoying your life now. It's also not okay to find people who are not right for you to fill the void of loneliness. It's not a tragedy being alone. Take this time to be selfish and enjoy doing whatever you want without worrying about anyone else but you!

Finding Comfort Alone

Do you ever sit alone in a café, or does that make you nervous? Are you constantly surrounded by other people, so you won't have to be alone with your own thoughts? Do you always find yourself jumping from one relationship to another one, when one ends? If you believe these scenarios apply to you, then you need to work on loving yourself more and building a better relationship with you! It is so important to take this opportunity to discover yourself. Get busy enjoying any hobbies you want to try. Plan all the girl's nights you want. Plan dates and get to know what you want out of a relationship without having any expectations of how the date will turn out. Go out and try shopping and dining alone. Discover what you love to wear without hearing the opinions of others. Try sitting in a coffee shop alone, doing some work, or reading a book, even if it may feel a little awkward at first for you. Take self-development classes online or start a journal to understand yourself better. It's so important to go through this phase, so you don't ever lose who you are when you are in a relationship.

Enjoying the Single Life

If you are single, this is the best time, and only time, you have to truly use your freedom to do whatever you want. When you have a partner or children, your lifestyle will naturally change. You will have new responsibilities. You won't have as much time for yourself anymore. It will be a completely different lifestyle. So, take advantage of this phase of your life, because once you find your soulmate, you won't have this life again. This is the time to travel, take classes, and to really find yourself and what you love. Don't get me wrong, you can do the same when you are married and have children. However, doing things alone is a different experience, that will bring adventure to your life in a totally different way, then when you have your own family. You want to avoid getting to the point of regret where you say to yourself, "I wish I took more advantage of my single days." Or "wish I spent my time alone wisely." Write down all your goals and dreams that you want to accomplish and start working on them right now! As you become busy enjoying your life, your soulmate will come out of nowhere and ask to become a part of your happy life. Just be patient.

DATING RULES:

While you are dating, there are some rules to keep in mind to find the right person for your life. Enjoy every moment of the dating process when you decide to date.

1. **Enjoy dating and learn from the person you are dating. Learn what you do and don't like for your life long relationship. You can even learn from only one date with a person.**
2. **Do not imagine each person you are dating, as the one you are going to marry. This attitude will be felt by the person you are going out with. You will end up giving off the vibe of neediness, which will turn them off.**

3. If you are dating and not exclusive with anyone, keep your options open to anyone who is interested in you. This will prevent you from getting attached to anyone that hasn't promised you an exclusive relationship yet. Once someone asks you to be exclusive with them and you are open to the idea, go ahead and stop the dating process with others.
4. Have fun on your dates! Enjoy your time. See this as an opportunity to get to know yourself better.
5. Don't chase any guy! It's a turn off to them.
6. Until you get comfortable with yourself and being alone, you won't truly know if you are choosing someone when your dating out of love, or out of loneliness.

Romantic Relationships

(Keep the Spark Alive)

"Two are better than one" – Ecclesiastes 4:9

Finding your soulmate and going through life with him is the most beautiful journey you can take with a person. Sharing your laughs, your tears, your space, your dreams, your goals, and your whole life with someone you choose to love for the rest of your life is magical. Unfortunately, a lot of times, this magic may get lost or disappear at certain phases in our lives. Relationships may go downhill after getting comfortable and knowing each other for so long. Those butterflies you used to get in your stomach may disappear. Each person in the relationship takes the other for granted and blame each other for changing. You may settle with the idea that the sparks don't last forever, and the exciting love disappears after a while. But that's only true if you believe this is true. If you work on your relationship every day, your love will grow stronger and deeper. You can feel the butterflies in your stomach again. And you can keep the magical sparks in your relationship forever.

Let's assume you are in a healthy relationship. A healthy relationship means you are with a person who loves you, is committed to you, and does not involve himself in bad habits or addictions, like abuse, cheating, gambling, alcohol etc. However, you have been together for a while, and the spark in your relationship is going downhill, or maybe it's even lost. The first thing you might want to do is blame your man. However, let's dismiss the blaming game and focus on ourselves first. Yes, there may be some blame on him. But remember, a relationship takes two. Let's fix your part first, and he most likely will see the effort and will be inspired to put the effort in as well. So, what can you do to bring that spark back into your love life? (For simplicity's sake, marriage will mostly be the example given. However, this advice goes for anyone, including committed or long-term relationships.)

"Do what you did at the beginning of a relationship and there won't be an end." - Anthony Robbins

A Woman's Attraction

Before marriage, women are usually busy enjoying their lives. Think back to your single or dating life. Maybe you used to dress up every day and do your hair and makeup every morning. You planned girls' nights out often. You went to the gym after work. You took a cooking class on the weekends. You traveled often. You were always seen smiling, laughing, and welcomed life with open arms. You seemed so ambitious and happy. When you were out enjoying life, minding your own business, you caught your soulmate's attention, and he fell in love with you. Now think about your relationship with your hubby when you were dating or engaged. Did you show your appreciation and excitement more when he bought you something or did something for you? Did you say *"please and thank you"* to him all the time? Were you more patient with him? Did you communicate your feelings to him in a mature way without yelling at him or giving him a bad attitude, when you were unhappy? Did you used to show him how excited you were to see him more than you do now? Everything was so magical! Why does it disappear? When we enter a long-term relationship, we start to focus more on relationship demands and responsibilities. Along the way, we forget about ourselves and put our romantic relationship on the back burner. We have to go to work. Make more money. Clean the house and get the laundry done. We have to pick up after the household. Plan family events. Deal with daily life struggles etc....Where did the real authentic you go in all of this? Where did your loving relationship with your partner go in all of this? It's true, being married and building a family takes a lot of your time. However, you need to also make time for yourself and your relationship with your partner. If you make it a priority you will find time for it. Learn to balance the chaos of life and also enjoy your time with your partner as well. Don't lose who you were before marriage. Remember, your man fell in love with you, when you were embracing life. That's why it's essential for you to learn how to be happy when you are single. Your single life prepares you for when you get sucked into family life; you still know how to be you. Go back to who you were and who your hubby fell in love with when he first met you. Light up your world again. The spark in your relationship will come back and stay when you work on it.

Open your Ears and Listen to Him

Here's the thing about listening. Not many people are good at it. There's a disconnection in the way humans communicate because there's an increase in talking and a lack of listening. It's like listening to music in the background, you hear it, but you don't pay attention to the lyrics. Sometimes, you may find yourself talking to a friend about a problem, but you feel she's not really listening. Her lips want to move and she wants to stop you from talking, so you can hear her own experience, or lecture you about what to do. We love to express ourselves and get attention and feel heard by others. However, when we talk too much, we release unnecessary information that shouldn't be shared or should have been kept in our private thoughts. This goes against the beauty of being mysterious Listening is a part of mystery that keeps people attracted to you, including men. Actually, especially men. Did you use to listen attentively and show your interest when he talks and tells you stories, and now you half-listen to what he says if you even listen at all? Maybe that's why he may not talk to you like he used to, and you wonder why you don't have deep conversations with each other anymore. Practice your listening skills with your partner. Really listen to what he is saying without creating thoughts in your mind about what you want to respond back. Make eye contact. Give off the energy that you are truly interested in what he is saying. This will magnetize him towards you. You will be wiser and more knowledgeable when you listen. You will be able to understand the actions behind his behavior when you hear his stories. You are respected more by him when you are not running your mouth and exposing every thought that comes to your mind. The next time your hubby comes home from work and wants to chat with you. Put down the dishes or whatever you are doing. Let him do more of the talking. Watch how he will become more magnetized by you, just because your eyes are on him and your body position shows him you're giving him all your attention. And your smile attracts him while he talks. Learn to ask questions and listen to the answers you receive, instead of jumping to advise him or lecture him. Practice these skills with everyone around you as well. Lots of stories and curiosity unfold when you listen to people talk, and you discover so many details in people's lives that you were never aware of before. The more you practice the art of listening, the more you understand its power.

How to Get What you Want from Him

One of the most important parts for a successful marriage is communication. Learning how to communicate with your man will bring you happiness and will get you what you want in your relationship. The way you talk to your man will determine whether you will get what you want or end up fighting. Expressing your feelings and being vulnerable may not always be easy. You may worry about causing drama or looking too needy in front of him. However, you can learn to communicate your feelings and get what you want without causing yourself conflict with him.

First, you must remember something. You married this man because you make each other happy and you love each other. He is with you because he wants to make you happy. He is not out to get you or make you miserable. Men actually take great pleasure in making their women happy. It's all about how you approach him. There are two common mistakes we do when we communicate with our hubby. The first mistake is not communicating at all. You would rather hold a grudge against him when he forgets about your dinner plans together, instead of communicating your hurt feelings. The second mistake when communicating with him is by playing the blaming game. You tell him it's his fault for forgetting your dinner plans because he doesn't care and blah, blah, blah. You just want to point your finger at him when it's his mistake or when he upsets you. What you really need to learn is the third way of communication. The third way of communicating is by expressing your feelings in an adult way. Instead of not telling him how you feel or blaming him, try telling him you are sad he forgot and you are hurt because you were looking forward to spending time with him. Also try to understand why he may have forgotten about the plans. Maybe he had a bad day or is worried about something, keeping his brain busy. When you express your feelings, you don't blame him or criticize him. Most importantly, you expressed your feelings at the appropriate time, instead of bottling up your feelings and exploding later when you had enough. How can he argue with that? You are only telling him how you feel about the situation. Even if he tries to defend himself, don't argue. You already said how you feel, and he will find a way to solve the problem to make you happy again.

Drop Your Expectations

Here's the thing, when you marry your soulmate, you start to know each other so well that you think you know everything about him - from his shoe size to what his pet peeves are. You most likely live together so obviously you know everything about him, right? But do you really? It's so important in any relationship, especially your romantic one, to never assume anything, no matter how much you think you know him. On the contrary, you have the right to expect the basic characteristics of your hubby. These characteristics include: love, respect, trust, commitment, and support. However, we sometimes expect more from our spouse that leaves us disappointed and even resenting him. We may expect flowers on V-day. We may expect him to know what makes us happy and what makes us upset. We expect him to remember there's no milk at home, and he should pick it up after work. We expect him to know what we want for our birthday. It's the expectation that he can read your mind, and you can read his that makes trouble in a relationship. To avoid this trouble, tell him in a kind and direct way your needs and wants. He will be more than happy for you to tell him what you need, rather than him trying to guess. Keep in mind both of you have responsibilities, worries, feelings, stress, and much more that you deal with during the day. Expecting too much from each other would just be unfair.

Do You Appreciate What You Expect?

Let's say your hubby takes you to the movies twice a month. He has been taking you to the movies ever since you started dating. Do you still get excited for movie night as much as the first time he took you? Do you at least show him appreciation for keeping the tradition going? If the answer is no, then you really need to stop expecting much from him. This is his way of showing you he loves you, appreciates spending time with you, and keeps the spark in your relationship going. If you "expect" him to take you out but don't show as much enthusiasm or appreciation, he will think it is hard to please you and stop putting in the effort. If you really don't enjoy going to the movies any more than communicate that with him, without hurting his feelings. You can say something like, *"I love that we get to spend time together at the movies. However, I would like to change the routine a bit. What do you think we should do?"* This way, you don't hurt his feelings and make the mistake of saying you're bored of going to the movies with him! He may even be happy you brought up the subject and he also may be ready for another date night routine!

Appreciate Everything. Expect Nothing

As mentioned previously, you should expect in your relationship love, support, trust, respect, and commitment. However, let's stop putting pressure on people and expecting anything from them, including our spouses. Let's go back to the way you were when you first met each other. When he bought you flowers randomly, jump up and down, and give him a big hug for thinking of you. When he takes out the trash, give him a kiss to show him appreciation. When he buys you a gift, show him how happy and surprised you are for his kind gesture. Be careful not to hurt his feelings when he buys something or does something for you. If he gets you the wrong colored bracelet, swallow your tongue and appreciate the gift, instead of scolding him about how it's the wrong colored bracelet. If you do this, you will probably not get many gifts from him after that. Make sure you show him lots of appreciation for anything he does for you. If you show little to no appreciation, you will notice a pattern of him doing less and less because he may be feeling confused and hurt for not being able to please you. Lastly, if you need something or want something, either ask him kindly, and directly, or do what you need yourself. It's true that we can lean on our spouse for support and help. However, we are individuals as well, and we should be taking care of our needs and wants ourselves. No one wants the responsibility of having someone fully dependent on them. Take care of yourself, show appreciation in everything your hubby does for you, and stop expecting the unexpected.

"It's not a lack of love, but a lack of friendship that makes unhappy marriages." – Frederich Nietzsche

Elevate your Relationship

So how do you elevate your relationship with your partner? How do you bring romance back into your life? What will bring back the spark again? Let's stop keeping score of who's doing what and love from our hearts. Put in your effort, and be patient for him to start making changes as well. Go back to the late-night deep talks you used to have. Go back to joking and pranking each other. Go back to dressing up and making an effort for him again. Go back to appreciating what he does for you. Go back to being interested and attentive in what he says, what he likes, and what makes him happy. Enjoy and be present in the moment you are with each other, and don't take it for granted. Enjoy giving each other time apart and space with your own friends and hobbies, so you both don't lose your individuality. Never laugh or make fun of each other in front of people. Never put each other down. You are a team. You are not against each other. Always defend each other even if someone throws "a joke" at your partner. Defend him. This will really strengthen your relationship. Never talk badly about each other to anyone. Even if your friend complains about little things like how her husband never helps in the house. Do no expose your man's imperfections. That's part of respect. Do not compete with each other in anything. Again, you are a team! Don't be spoiled and selfish. A relationship is the total opposite of selfish. A spoiled woman drags along all the unattractive traits like nagging, complaining, drama, and unappreciation. No man wants a girl who acts spoiled, and only thinks of herself. And lastly, don't get comfortable in your relationship!

Speaking of comfort...

Being too comfortable with each other can make your intimacy disappear without you realizing it. Think about it like this: When a guy sees a woman dressed up, laughing, and having a good time, he is intrigued by her and finds her very attractive. If he is able to catch her interest as well and takes her out, she will show her best self. Even if something about her not so glamorous life comes up, she won't make it look so bad. Obviously, a long-term relationship is way deeper than that. But, the first few encounters with a man actually hold one of the secrets to keeping the spark alive. It's the mystery! Our inner emotions, negativity, and imperfections should be dealt with between ourselves and not projected onto our spouse. Yes, he may accept the way you are no matter what, but it could degrade the spark between each other. Let's say you have an anger problem and tried to manage it as best you could while you were getting to know each other. Now that you're married and feel more comfortable with each other, your short temper gets more exposed. You may believe he should love you just the way you are and life is tough anyway! You can't control your anger anymore! Well, that's not fair to him or your relationship for you to think and act like that. Your anger issue needs to be dealt with on your own or even with a professional. Yes, your husband loves you no matter what. But to keep the spark going and stay mysterious in his eyes, you must work on and manage your negativity and imperfections between yourself. Shut the bathroom door. Don't share details of your acne problem. Keep your stress under control around him. Save your old lady pajamas for sick days and pull out the cute ones he loves to see you in and wear them. He doesn't need to know how long it's been since you washed your hair. He also doesn't need to watch you pull out your nose hairs. Basically, keep that mystery about you alive in front of his eyes and don't get too comfortable in front of him!

Overall Recap!

Don't forget to…

Talk kindly to each other. Even when you are having a disagreement, do it respectfully. Don't point your finger at him, blame him, and criticize him. Instead, communicate your feelings and solve the issues together. Do not purge your imperfections and negativity on to him. It's so unattractive. Find a therapist for that. Don't let everyday stress, responsibilities, and obstacles interfere with your relationship. Sometimes everyday life takes over, and we put romance on the back burner not realizing our relationship will catch on fire this way. Forgive, Forgive, Forgive. Your spouse married you because he loves you. He does not want to hurt you or be your enemy. He wants you both to be a team together. So, forgive your man for any hurt he has caused you in the past, or any miscommunications that happens between the two of you. And lastly, whenever you feel your losing your spark in your relationship again, go back to the way you were when you first met. The way you behaved, dressed, and lived your life. Usually, those are some of the funnest years in a person's life anyways. Your relationship with your man is like no other in this world. You have a best friend for life plus all the fun intimacy benefits. You have a promise from another human being to love you, respect you, support you, and commit to you for life. Don't take for granted the one who promised to stick by you for life. Show him your love, your appreciation, your kindness, your selflessness, and your positive attitude that you will both enjoy and get through your journey in life together, happily, and successfully without putting out the sparks between the two of you.

Enjoy your Relationship Benefits

Please enjoy the benefits of your relationship and never take it for granted. Receiving unexpected gifts. Having a shoulder to cry on. Having a support system for your dreams and goals. Intimacy. Movie nights. Date nights. Snuggly Sundays. A soulmate who will stand by you in your darkest days. A soulmate who lives with you through your happiest moments. Vacationing together. Laughing together. Making fun inside jokes together. Doing fun hobbies together. Forgive each other constantly for being human. And let your love bring you together stronger, closer, and deeper.

Who Inspires You to Elevate Your Life?

"Surround yourself with people who challenge you, teach you, and push you to be your best self." -Bill Gates

Did you ever meet someone who gives you this electric jolt through your body to be the best version of yourself just by talking to them? Maybe she lives in your town, and she owns a jewelry store. She lives alone with her cat. And she has the most impressive social life you have ever seen. Have you ever met someone by chance and say something to you that made you think not twice, but three times about your perception of life? Maybe you're at school, and your professor decided to share with you her life story about how she went from a low point in her life to becoming a millionaire, and you had no idea all semester that your professor is actually a very special person with a special story behind her. Did you ever experience yourself following someone from a distance? Maybe you follow a fitness influencer on Instagram who is Vegan with five dogs and travels all over the world. Or maybe she is a YouTube influencer who is a doctor and also has her own clothing line on the side. You watch these women from afar but get inspired in your own life to be the best you possible. You may notice these people often come into our lives at the time we need them most and leave our life when we have learned and grown from them. As long as you keep your eye out for those who inspire you, become aware of their inspiration, and breathe it into your own life, you will be able to feed off of their energy to elevate your life. That's why it is important to minimize the ones who drain you, who are full of drama and do nothing for your soul. You want to make as much room as possible in your life, for the ones that give you the motivation to jump out of bed and be the best version of you!

Who is Inspiring you?

(My Own Experience)

I have this radiant friend. She is the definition of happiness. I always questioned her about her life and what she did over the weekend to learn more about her lifestyle. She is married with two dogs and a cat. She mostly cooked at home and went to the gym three days a week. Her and her husband paid off all their debt and live very simple lives. She never really went shopping, and if she did, she would buy her things mostly at the thrift store. Her clothes always looked put together and classy but extremely simple. She only bought and kept what she needed. She always carried a variety of teas and a silver fork in her lunch box so she would limit the use of plastic. She only wore brown eyeliner and mascara. She had some skin issues she was sometimes self-conscious about, but she didn't realize how much her face glowed, and no one paid attention to her insecurities. She fully enjoyed going out to restaurants when she had the chance with her husband, which wasn't too often since she cooked and meal planned mostly at home. She had the worst work schedule that clashed with her husband's work schedule. However, she didn't really complain and made it work for her lifestyle. She never complained at work and had a very efficient work ethic. Whenever she needed any help at work, her co-workers were always ready to jump in and help. She has a very sweet and bubbly personality. She lives in the present only and faces the day as it comes. She doesn't hold grudges, and she is very understanding with people. However, you could catch her fume at times and then laugh it off or forget about the situation that made her mad shortly after. As simple as she was, she just had a beautiful, radiant, and healthy glow to her. She was always happy and made you happy when you are around her. After knowing her for almost two years, God made her dreams come true.

Her husband's job relocated him to the same state her parents live in. Her life was full of satisfaction and content. Miracles were always working in her favor. However, I learned it wasn't just because luck was on her side but more because she appreciated her daily life. She only got what she needed, and everything else was an extra treasure. She was always grateful in any situation she was in, including her troubles and not so great situations. She also put her faith in God, that whatever she cannot control, she believed He would take care of her.

I had another inspiring person enter my life. She was my personal instructor during school. When I first met her, I was so drawn by her appearance. She was such a pretty petite Armenian/Russian girl in her early 30s. I learned quickly that she was married with a one-year-old daughter and leaving for surgery in a month for a double mastectomy due to breast cancer. I couldn't believe that this cute, pretty girl who lost her mom to breast cancer at age 11 and going into surgery in a month, appeared to have life under control and appeared beyond elegant in her looks and the way she carried herself. I had only known her for a few weeks before she left for a few months. When she finally came back to be my instructor again, I was able to learn more about her as a person. I loved the way her hair was always neatly tied or neatly flowing to her shoulders. She had an impeccable posture. Her makeup was always done using natural brown tones eye shadows with shimmer and small, winged eyeliner. She was always careful about watching what she ate. Her health was very important to her. She hated shopping, but she always wore cute and fashionable items. When I went to her house the first time, I noticed her house had all the rooms she needed and nothing too extra. The house décor was pretty and neat but extremely simple as well. Her closet was small, but every outfit was cute and fashionable. She loves wearing heels and fun earrings. Her makeup consisted of a makeup bag and a small drawer in the bathroom. At work, she was always making her daily, weekly, and monthly to-do lists. She was always professional, neat, and gave her best at work. Her personality was very intriguing. She was strong, sassy, and sarcastic. She was good at saying the funniest comments with a straight face.

She knew when to speak up and say what she wants and when to just let things go. She loves reading books and listening to podcasts or inspirational speeches to keep her motivated in life. Anytime she was in an unhappy state, she would work hard at changing her situation and never settle for unhappiness. Despite all she has been through and the difficulty of her past, she glowed in her life, and everyone loved her and her sassy attitude.

There are a few common characteristics that these two women share. They both live simple lives and know that materialistic things enhance their life, but are not the source of happiness. I find it interesting that they both entered my life at a time when they were going through difficult situations or not so pleasant circumstances. I was able to watch how graceful they lived their lives through tough times. I was also able to witness how they both elevated their lives for the better when they were unhappy with any situation they were in. They both had patience. They did not complain or make drama of their circumstance. And they worked quietly on changing whatever circumstance they were unhappy with. Be aware of when people who are elevators enter your life. Observe these extraordinary people and get inspired by them to live your best life. You also need to be aware of when energy drainers and dramatic people enter your life as well.

Sometimes the people we love and see every day are our energy drainers. We are all on different journeys and different levels of mindset. As difficult as it may be, don't be afraid to let go of people that are not bringing value to your life. Instead, fill your life with inspiration, whether its people you know personally or someone you find on social media or a book that motivates you. Wherever your inspiration comes from, search for it, and surround your life with whoever and whatever elevates you to the fullest.

A Purpose for Life -Faith

"To trust in God in the light is nothing, but trust Him in the dark – that is faith." -C.H.S Purgeon

• Even if you're not religious, just read! It won't hurt you!

It's impossible to write this book without mentioning the importance of having faith in a higher power. Faith is what keeps you from collapsing in your weakest moments in life. Faith is what gives you comfort and strength when you feel confused, alone, hopeless, anxious, worried, or sad. There's a secret to religion and why people pray to God. The secret is feeling the power and presence of God in your personal life. That's the reason why people keep praying and continue to believe in Him. Prayer gives you the opportunity to believe that miracles do happen. When a person prays about their troubles and their prayers are answered, they know that God is what gave them their strength. When a person feels lonely, and the loneliness disappears after they pray, that gives them comfort. When a person is grateful in life, and they pray in gratitude, they will feel a sense of joy run through their body that is unexplainable. Developing a relationship between you and God will bring you the most happiness in life.

God is Love – 1 John 4:8

The beautiful thing about God is He loves everyone and welcomes everyone to have a relationship with Him. Whether you are poor, rich, alone, happy, sad, gay, single, divorced, you didn't believe in Him before, or you have done some regretful things in the past. It doesn't matter who you are or where you are from. He accepts all of us just the way we are. He knows we are imperfect and that we will do many horrible things in our life. However, as John 3:16 states, *"God so loved the world, that He gave His only Son up for sacrifice, so our sins would be forgiven."* So never feel inferior, or you are not worth anything to Him, because of your imperfections. As long as you have faith that He will stand by you, and deliver your prayers throughout your life, He will be there. Proverbs 8:17 reassures us how God feels about us. *"I love those who love me and those who seek me diligently find me."* All you have to do is want Him in your life, and you will find Him there. Just be patient because God is patience. *"The Lord is not slow about His promise as some count slowness, but is patient toward you"* – 2Peter 3:9. Even if you have not found God, or do not believe he can be part of your life, He is present waiting for you to "seek" Him. If you always feel like there is an unfulfilled or empty part of your life, try to see if believing in a higher power who is rooting for us to win life's journey, may fill that empty gap for you. Be sure to have faith because, without it, your journey in life will be more difficult.

Psalm 23:4 – *"Even though I walk through the darkest valley. I will fear no evil, for you are with me; Your rod and your staff, they comfort me."*

The Power of Prayer

Praying to God will give you this instant release of heavy bricks from your shoulders and heart. Prayer can be thought of like a diary or journal. You pour out your heart about anything, from the good in your life that you are grateful for, and the bad that keeps you up at night, worried and anxious. You can pray about your day. Pray about a problem. Pray for strength. Pray for the world. You can pray about anything. You can also pray any time you want to. You can even pray out loud or inside your heart (He will hear your silent prayer as well). With prayer and faith, you will notice a difference in your emotions, like a feeling of comfort and contentment. The more you pray and have your own personal relationship with God, the more you will see miracles in your life. You will be in disbelief when you see what you prayed for is turning into a reality, especially when what you prayed for looks impossible and unattainable. The more you pray, the more comfortable you will feel doing it. The more you pray, the more you will also feel that there is a life beyond this concrete world. You will experience and see the extraordinary world of the unseen. The more you pray, the less you will worry, and the more you will be content in your life. You will experience less fear and more feelings of a sense of relief and hope. Prayer will give you a life more beautiful and meaningful to you.

Talking about God as part of our happiness is an encouragement for you to explore this part of life you may never have experienced before. Or it may be an encouragement to go deeper into this part of your life that you haven't been able to give more time and effort to. The more you witness in your life, the power of prayer and your relationship with God without giving up, the more willing you will feel that anything is possible and you can get through anything in life. Remember, no matter who you are, what you have done in your past, and what you are doing right now, everyone is accepted and wanted by Him. Leave your guilt, shame, and worries behind and tell Him everything. It's okay to be uncomfortable while you pray just like you would feel with a new acquaintance. You will eventually build that relationship up and talk to Him like a best friend. Keep your faith strong. And keep praying on.

This chapter encourages you to try to build a relationship with God and to believe in the power that is beyond this world and have faith in the unseen. Once you believe and have faith in the higher power, life will show you a world that you have never experienced before. You may want to explore this part of your life if you have never experienced it before. This chapter also encourages you to go deeper into this part of your life if you haven't been able to give more time and effort to your relationship with Him, if you already believe in Him.

Your Journey Has Just Begun…

Hey there happy lady…

You have reached the end of this book, but only have begun your journey to choosing happiness every day. Apply what you have learned to your life daily. Remember, no matter how many happiness books you read, if you don't do the work, you're not going to improve anything. It's not just about learning the information. It's how you apply it in your life as well. You are the artist of your life. You can design your life, the way you want to live it every day. Inspire others around you to make a difference in their lives by being their example. Don't give up on creating happiness in your everyday life. It will definitely be harder on some days…or weeks…or months… It will take lots of self-control to minimize your anger, fears, jealousy, and hurt. It will take awareness to be the bigger person and turn any negativity to positivity. It will take effort to get up, dress up, and take care of your health and body. But you have the tools, the ambition, and the heart to create your daily happiness. Don't forget to let yourself feel your emotions without always reacting to them. There is so much beauty in this world. Go and follow this beauty that attracts you to be alive every day. Tune out everything else that's negative and uninspiring. Your happiness is only in your hands. Create your own happiness bubble that no one is allowed to burst for you. As long as your bubble is floating in the air with you inside dancing to your own song, nothing around you will affect you. And lastly, Forgive…Forgive…Forgive… Forgive others and forgive yourself for any mistakes that are made along the way of your journey. Your love for yourself and your love for life is more than enough to give the world and others around you. Choose your happiness daily!

CPSIA information can be obtained
at www.ICGtesting.com
Printed in the USA
LVHW030446240520
656397LV00004B/526